Mobility of Light
The Poetry of Nicole Brossard

A Bilingual Publication

Selected
with an
introduction by
Louise H. Forsyth
and an
afterword by
Nicole Brossard

lps
LAURIER POETRY SERIES

Wilfrid Laurier University Press
WLU

We acknowledge the support of the Canada Council for the Arts for our publishing program. We acknowledge the financial support of the Government of Canada through the Book Publishing Industry Development Program for our publishing activities.

Catalogage avant publication de Bibliothèque et Archives Canada

Brossard, Nicole, 1943–
[Poèmes. Anglais & français. Morceaux choisis]
   Mobility of light : the poetry of Nicole Brossard / selected with an introduction by Louise H. Forsyth and an afterword by Nicole Brossard.

(Laurier poetry series)
Texte original français et traduction anglaise sur pages en regard.
ISBN 978-1-55458-047-7

   I. Forsyth, Louise   II. Titre.   III. Titre: Poèmes. Anglais & français. Morceaux choisis. IV. Collection: Laurier poetry series

PS8503.R7A2 2009   C841'.54   C2009-900703-7F

Library and Archives Canada Cataloguing in Publication

Brossard, Nicole, 1943–
[Poems. English & French. Selections]
   Mobility of light : the poetry of Nicole Brossard / selected with an introduction by Louise H. Forsyth and an afterword by Nicole Brossard.

(Laurier poetry series)
Original French text with English translation on facing pages.
ISBN 978-1-55458-047-7

   I. Forsyth, Louise   II. Title.   III. Title: Poems. English & French. Selections.   IV. Series: Laurier poetry series

PS8503.R7A2 2009   C841'.54   C2009-900703-7E

Table of Contents

Foreword

At the beginning of the twenty-first century, poetry in Canada—writing and publishing it, reading and thinking about it—finds itself in a strangely conflicted place. We have many strong poets continuing to produce exciting new work, and there is still a small audience for poetry; but increasingly, poetry is becoming a vulnerable art, for reasons that don't need to be rehearsed.

But there are things to be done: we need more real engagement with our poets. There needs to be more access to their work in more venues—in classrooms, in the public arena, in the media—and there need to be more, and more different kinds, of publications that make the wide range of our contemporary poetry more widely available.

The hope that animates this series from Wilfrid Laurier University Press is that these volumes help to create and sustain the larger readership that contemporary Canadian poetry so richly deserves. Like our fiction writers, our poets are much celebrated abroad; they should just as properly be better known at home.

Our idea is to ask a critic (sometimes herself a poet) to select thirty-five poems from across a poet's career; write an engaging, accessible introduction; and have the poet write an afterword. In this way, we think that the usual practice of teaching a poet through eight or twelve poems from an anthology is much improved upon; and readers in and out of classrooms will have more useful, engaging, and comprehensive introductions to a poet's work. Readers might also come to see more readily, we hope, the connections among, as well as the distances between, the life and the work.

It was the ending of an Al Purdy poem that gave Margaret Laurence the epigraph for *The Diviners*: "but they had their being once/and left a place to stand on." Our poets still do, and they are leaving many places to stand on. We hope that this series helps, variously, to show how and why this is so.

—*Neil Besner*
General Editor

Biographical Note

Nicole Brossard was born in Montréal in 1943. She completed a *Licence ès lettres* and the coursework for a master's degree at the Université de Montréal and a *Baccalauréat spécialisé en pédagogie* at the Université du Québec à Montréal. Montréal has always been her home. She began her career as a radical poet and theorist early in her student years and was quickly recognized as a bold and innovative voice during those revolutionary years when Quebec was re-thinking its ideas about sexuality, values, its language, its identity, its place in Canada and the world. In 1965 Brossard published her first poetry collection, *Aube à la saison*, and in 1966 co-founded the influential and long-lived literary magazine *La Barre du Jour.*

The following decades were years in which she was inspired by feminist consciousness and lesbian utopia. In 1976 she co-directed with Luce Guilbeault the NFB film *Some American Feminists* and was involved in the feminist play *La nef des sorcières*, for which she wrote the monologue "L'écrivain." That same year, she co-founded the feminist newspaper *Les Têtes de pioche.* Her radical essay *La lettre aérienne* was published in English translation in 1988. During those years Brossard's writing evolved through the analysis of patriarchy. She renewed her relationship to language and transformed her approach to meaning, fiction, reality, and the notion of values.

Brossard is the author of more than thirty poetry collections and chapbooks, ten novels, a dramatic monologue, a documentary film, four books of essays, and countless theoretical articles. She has prepared four groundbreaking anthologies of poetry. Among these was *Anthologie de la poésie des femmes au Québec*, the first of its kind, which she co-edited in 1991 with Lisette Girouard. This anthology has since appeared in an enlarged second edition.

Brossard's poetry and novels have been translated and widely circulated in nine languages. Her work has figured regularly in anthologies around the world in many languages. Her poetry has twice received the Governor General's Literary Award and was shortlisted on three more

occasions. She has twice received the Grand Prix de Poésie du Festival International de Trois-Rivières. *Notebook of Roses and Civilization,* the translation of *Cahier de roses et de civilisation,* was recently shortlisted for the Griffin Prize for Poetry. Brossard is the recipient of two honorary doctorates and is a member of l'Académie des Lettres du Québec and the Royal Society of Canada. Some of the other prestigious awards she has received include the B.P. Nichol Chapbook Award, the Prix Athanase-David, the Harbourfront Festival Prize, the W.O. Mitchell Prize, the Bourse de carrière du Conseil des Arts et des Lettres du Québec, and the Canada Council Molson Prize.

Always sensitive to receiving signs from that which is real yet *ailleurs,* Brossard is an inveterate local and global traveller. She has participated in conferences, undertaken lecture tours, delivered keynote talks, served as writer-in-residence, and read in festivals. Beginning in the 1960s, she has organized major conferences for writers in Quebec and elsewhere.

Nicole Brossard has been read by three generations of poets and readers who have acknowledged the importance of her work. For it seems that there are always emotional, intellectual, and sensual sparks that fly when people who love words gather and share her thoughts and ardour. The sounds of poetry are everywhere that Nicole Brossard puts her energy. She has dedicated herself to the understanding of the materials human beings are made of and, mostly, of what really matters in us that renews hope and lust.

More information on the personal and professional life of Nicole Brossard can be found in *Journal intime; L'horizon du fragment;* and "Autobiography," in *Fluid Arguments,* pages 117–45. The latter appeared originally as "Nicole Brossard 1943–," translated by Susanne de Lotbinière-Harwood, in *Contemporary Authors Autobiography Series,* vol. 16 (1992), pages 39–57.

Introduction

Poetic Firewords at the Speed of Light

To be a poet is to place pleasure, beauty and sensual delights front and centre, it means having a predilection for debauchery. –Nicole Brossard[1]

Nicole Brossard magically calls forth secrets from words and launches these words with the mobility of light into the minds and bodies of her readers.[2] From the start of her illustrious career as a bold experimental writer, a focus on the power of language has determined the many trajectories of her art. Language is much more than a simple medium for communication. In fact, communication is never simple in Brossard's texts, for her relations with readers are not presumed to be based on the model of an active sender and a passive receiver. The dynamic exchange that occurs in the moment her poetry is read implies a shared process in the creation of meaning and the simultaneous coexistence of subjects on both sides of the white page. In Brossard's oeuvre, language is so all-encompassing that it is coterminous with and inseparable from the being of humanity itself: "Our humanity is in letters and symbols, our comfort in figures and signs."[3] The impact of the intensity of Brossard's passion for language used with the energy and vision needed to capture life in its rich integrality is, quite simply, dazzling. Words that previously seemed banal to readers suddenly reveal themselves to be *indocile*; readers join Brossard at the centre of modern cities in her feminist and ludic modes where she positions herself as intractably *insoumise* insofar as received social myths, lies deriving from discursive clichés, and abuses of power are concerned.

The poet's reflections on what writing and language mean to her—while she sees herself alone in the Barcelona labyrinth in the nearby presence of hundreds of women, many lesbians—capture eloquently the ardent creative writer's vocation that has driven her for more than four decades:

> i am writing this text on several levels because reality is not sufficient, because beauty is demanding, because sensations are multiple, because putting a great

deal of oneself into language does not eliminate the patriarchal horror, does not explain the composition of my subjectivity and all these images that move like a woman in orgasm. Energized by the raw material of desire, I write. Word [...] matter that is eternally contemporary with our joys and energized bodies, murmurs and breathes, opens us to the bone and sews in wells and depths of astonishment. I exist in written language because it is there that I decide the thoughts that settle the questions and answers I give to reality. [Language] is a fertile ground of vestiges and vertigo. Depository of illusions, of obsessions, of passions, of anger and *quoi encore* that obliges us to transpose reality.[4]

Brossard's writing practice relies heavily on language's performative function. Her words almost always suggest the theatricality of the world and of human performances in it, as is explicitly explored in the collection *Downstage Vertigo* (*Vertige de l'avant-scène*). The voice in many of her texts casts a detached, jaded, ironic, or angry eye on the performances of those who control culture's prevailing discourses and who have collectively constructed the illusion that their actions in the patriarchal and ethnocentric fictions they have imagined constitute unproblematic *reality*. Brossard ignites the magical power of words to subvert such *normal* understandings and literally produce alternative meanings. Her poems and other texts function performatively, in complicity with readers, to make new things happen and so actually change subjectivity and the world. *To write is heavy with consequences.* Even further, as is eloquently demonstrated in her texts since the early 1970s, when she positioned herself as a lesbian woman and feminist writer, "To write: I am a woman is heavy with consequences."[5]

Brossard's writing practice seems to set words free to roam and make multiple connections. Her words are like autonomous and mobile sparks, highly charged with polysemic energy. They are mysterious fragments of hidden yet virtual worlds. They work together to open that tantalizing space between one page and the next. They resemble the smallest shard of a holographic plate, each piece of which contains all the information necessary to reconstitute the entire plate. Yet glimpses of the virtual worlds contained in the sparks and shards are always transitory. Even for the poet, words are inevitably inadequate to capture definitively the fullness of elusive realities: "reality always exists elsewhere" ("Reality," from *Installations*). Just when one thinks to hold it, it slips away: "the universe is on the page one page over" ("Theatre. Speed of Water," from *Museum of Bone and Water*).

The magic of Brossard's words and the images they evoke stems from intense presence to her own corporeality, rationality, emotionality, spirituality, and materiality. In an often repeated affirmation, the poet insists that she is completely there in the present enunciative moment, at the moment the words of the poem are doing their work: "I am a woman of the present; that is what I have always been" ("Fragments of a Conversation," 32). It is not possible to find identitary coherence and construct the meanings of memories of the past, desires for the future, present experiences and emotions, thoughts about much that is absent but present in the mind unless one is intensely and lucidly present in the moment, in one's body and in a particular place. Silence is a necessary companion to presence. The richness of the virtual horizons offered by words can be experienced only if the silence surrounding the shapes, sounds, rhythms, meanings, and connotations of the words is heeded. The noise and the *common sense* of the world need to be blocked out so that one can hear and respond creatively to "the sounds of silence." Brossard has written recently of the dynamic and vital resources available "in the mysterious choreography of words on a backdrop of silence constituted by inner space."[6] The "vast complication of beauty" of which the poet speaks in *Harmonious Matter Is Still Manoeuvring* is vertiginously perceptible at moments of such ardent intensity in the present moment.

*

In the effervescent 1960s, when Brossard published her first volumes of poetry and co-founded *La Barre du Jour*, many in Quebec were angrily turning their backs on debilitating monolithic structures of traditional ideologies, throwing open doors on the modern world and shouting their legitimacy in claiming language for themselves, affirming their own sexuality, their autonomous presence in the world, and their right to unencumbered agency. It was a revolutionary time of passionate and erotic creativity in poetry and song. Brossard, like most poets of this generation, was committed to Quebec's independence and preservation of its unique language and culture. This commitment led many poets to write on themes of secular nationalism and produce images of *Terre Québec*.[7] Others, with Brossard, were poets of the modern city, poets of modernity choosing to use language reflectively rather than referentially. For them, language was an inexhaustible source of words to challenge powerful ideologically determined linguistic codes that control perceptions and behaviours: "the code struts / the code analyses the code

dictates" (*Suite logic*). Brossard was quickly seen to be a bold leader of these formalist poets, who have since been recognized as having breathed new life and vision into Quebec's language and literature.

The exchanges and debates among these poets and their *chansonnier* colleagues, whether identified primarily with nationalist or formalist streams, produced a large body of poetic work in Quebec of amazing originality. The culmination of the initial tidal wave of poetic fervour was the first *nuit de la poésie* in 1970.[8] Brossard was among the poets who celebrated the languages, beats, and images of poetry throughout that night of enchantment. The fire that burned ardently for an autonomous, secular, francophone Quebec has never died. Brossard's own rich body of poetry, her founding of poetry magazines, her original approach to anthologizing, and her organizing of poetry events have made her a locally and internationally esteemed artist. The fiery and passionate attachment to integrity in the use of words and to justice that Brossard displayed from the beginning was intensified early in the 1970s as she positioned herself as a feminist thinker and radical lesbian artist.

*

Brossard explored through her first five collections what language and poetry meant to her as an artist and thinker. The first line of the first poem in the first collection, *Season Dawning* (*Aube à la saison*), expresses the luminous intensity generated by her total commitment to writing poetry: "On strands of light I am hanging poetry like garlands." Poetry is planted in the poet's body: "planted in my belly and my heart poetry is." She attaches herself to its strength and beauty: "I anchor myself on your coral." This statement is not meant in a symbolic or abstract sense. On the contrary, the creation of poetry entails the engagement of the body with the mind, spirit, and voice, casting off all external interpellation and so engaging in the deviance and debauchery that can entirely disrupt a conventional sense of reality. Poems are affirmations of the reality of vast inner fields to which its language provides access.

Each of the first five collections shapes its own poetic form as it pushes back the horizons of what poetry is in order to capture the echo of what lies hidden. As one of the first in Quebec to write prose poetry, Brossard transgressed without hesitation the boundaries separating prose and poetry, fiction and theory. Her work with language has continued to derive great energy from the tension between sombre, mediocre external reality and the delirium of ardent vision: "in those opaque times the sky was trailing so much delirium" (*Suite logic*). Brossard has frequently

addressed the terrible conflicts between the vertigo of glimpsing utopia and the darkness of contemplating the horrors of patriarchal reality. She created with *The White Centre* (*Le centre blanc*) the image that runs through her work, with powerful sexual and spiritual connotations, of "vertigo," "ecstasy," "jouissance," "excitation," "ardour." The image of the white centre is both a reflection of the eye of the seer and the vital source of white-hot energy that inspires her poetry: "that idea of white centre, zen body, luminous body which will soon be replaced by the words synapses, neurons, *cortex exubérant*, every circuit that produces dreams."[9]

Brossard's early and sustained stress on language has often led her to single out certain words as particularly highly charged, as she did in *Coursing through the Veins* (*Au présent des veines*)—"they are always the same words"—and most strikingly in *Installations*, where some of the complexities, anomalies, and contradictions of words are exhibited. These poems are like art installations around which readers are invited to stroll, reflecting upon what comes to mind as they change position and recognizing that there is no end to what the words might suggest: "Learn to float among words, symbols, nuances and forms"[10]

Although the nouns are first noticed in *Installations (with and without pronouns)*, the full title also draws attention to pronouns.[11] The play of pronouns throughout Brossard's work, with their incessant and often mystifying shifts, is endlessly fascinating. Particularly interested in the construction of subjectivity and identity, Brossard's primary theme in *Obscure Tongues* (*Langues obscures*) is the interrogation of the pronoun "I." The poet addresses the first-person pronoun as a "pure construction of dreams / pure marvel," "pure rhetoric." She knows that the enunciating "I" exists only as a grammatical convention and rhetorical device, certainly not as the foundation for ontological certainty about the self. Still, she is aware that every individual has a sense of an existing self that surpasses the contingencies of language structures when they use the pronoun. It is this integral, eccentric self, always seeking knowledge about the meaning of its existence, conjoining in mysterious ways sensations, emotions, consciousness, spirit, mind, soul, memory, and desire, that has the strength and vision to combat the lies prevailing in the world. In *Obscure Tongues*, Brossard calls this consciousness and sense of one's own unique coherence and temporal endurance *the soul's watchdog*. Brossard's entire oeuvre is a far-ranging exploration of and playing with what can be said when the rhetorical or lyrical "I"—that is, the "I" who is writing—engages in a dialogue with the empirical "I," the eccentric self who claims real existence in the world. She exploits in richly creative ways the power to

name afforded to the lyrical "I" by its enunciative position, and to exploit the performative function of language in the production of new realities. It is this seemingly lucid self who can reflect in words upon the empirical self's existence in the world.

Exploring what it means to use the pronoun "I" and to plunge into the knowledges revealed by *obscure tongues*, the voices in the collection challenge received notions and values regarding the meaning of subjectivity and identity when living and writing as a woman. This has been central in Brossard's work for more than three decades, as the voices in her poetry explore the meaning of every facet of human existence when, centrally, women's lives and women's experiences matter.

*

While pronouns in Brossard's first five collections indicate that the voices represented are female, gender is neither problematized nor made salient until 1973, when she published the angry theoretical text "Vaseline" in *La Barre du Jour*: "A grammar that has as a rule: the masculine prevails over the feminine must be transgressed."[12] The following year she published *Daydream Mechanics* (*Mécanique jongleuse*), where she boldly disrupted the automatic linguistic and thought flow produced by sexist rules of grammar. In 1975, she edited the first of what would be a series of special issues of *La Barre du Jour* on women writers, "Femme et langage," where her text "*E* muet mutant" proclaims the emergence of women out of enforced silence, the *mute e* declared to be *mutating* into subjectivity, agency, and solidarity through speech and writing.

Brossard's already radical poetry made a strikingly new turn on the course of its spiralling poetics with the publication of *L'amèr ou le chapitre effrité* in 1977, where the narrative voice declared itself to be in *combat* against universally held views of *motherhood* and where she passionately celebrated, knowing it would hold enormous shock value, the reality of "bodies of mothers entwined." This intense love and sexual passion between women is the foundational theme in *Amantes*, a beautifully original love poem where women engage in passionate sexual, intellectual, and spiritual intercourse. So intense is their shared jouissance—igniting radiant garlands of body, mind, soul, and voice all at once—that it unfolds into "excitation" and produces an "integral presence" that is equally central to *Picture Theory*, the novel Brossard published in the same period. The scenes of ecstasy in *Lovhers* become utopic bliss in a space, "Ma continent," where women enjoy wholeness, knowledge derives from women's experiences, reality is transformed by women writing, and they

enter the space of humanity together. The material and spatial dimension of women's presence in "Ma continent" reminds us that poetry has, for Brossard from the beginning of her career, been a vast territory in which to move. The poet as seer contemplates the woman "*bringing me into the world.*" The lovers are joined on their continent by many other women: "everywhere women kept watch in the only way plausible: beautiful and serious in their energy from spiral to spiral." The names of a long line of lesbian writers are invoked. Their texts affirm the reality of feminist intertextuality, a lineage of women thinkers and artists across space and time. *Green Night of Labyrinth Park* (*La nuit verte du Parc Labyrinthe*) is a similar celebration, in an entirely different mode, of love and complicity among women, of their spatial gathering and presence in the modern city, of the poet's affirmation of her sense of being and belonging in the community of those whom she calls *urban women radicals*.

In Brossard's lexicon, lesbians have particular characteristics as subjects and agents. Lesbians are not only women whose sexuality and desires are driven by their love for women. In their union with other women there is, at the time their bodies meet, a meeting of minds, tongues, and values and a shared passion to rid the world's cities of patriarchal and other abusive hegemonies. They are artists and activists working in ardent complicity to create new realities absolutely removed from heterosexual and hetero-normative structures, practices, and symbolic images. Brossard enunciates in several places in her work what she calls her "fetish sentence": "A lesbian who does not reinvent the world is a lesbian on the path to disappearance."[13] As women belonging entirely to themselves and as feminists in a state of revolt, lucidity, and utopia, these "urban radicals of writing in movement, change reality, call it back to the drawing board, the laboratory of thought. There, it is subjected to transformations essential to the survival of projects keeping us alive. Urban radicals cross cities and myths, meeting there all manner of women."[14]

As staged in *These Our Mothers, Lovhers* (*Amantes*), *Surfaces of Sense* (*Le sens apparent*), *Picture Theory, Mauve Desert* (*Le désert mauve*), *Green Night of Labyrinth Park*, and *Baroque at Dawn* (*Baroque d'aube*), the vertiginous ecstasy and potential transformative power of the embrace of female lovers are radical. In the fullness of their love for each other, they have embraced all of human existence. It is in this sense that Brossard has been taking her name into the patriarchal city and its institutions, assuming her full place there as an *urban radical* and a public intellectual. Her first city was Montréal, a fabulous character in her novel *French Kiss*

(1974). Since then she has travelled more and more widely, claiming all cities as havens where women can enjoy the fullness of being, particularly those that lie at the edge of oceans and rivers. Her journeys, as evoked in *I'm Leaving for Trieste* (*Je m'en vais à Trieste*), have been wide. These travels complement the travels in inner space to elsewheres that she has taken on the wings of drifts, aerial letters, imagination, dreams, vertigo, and bliss.

Poetry collections published by Brossard in the past decade are stunning for their beauty, richness of insight, and visions of change for human habitation on the planet. They are poems of love on wide-ranging trajectories for all members of the human species who know how to savour the pleasure of a fulgurating dawn, a passionate embrace, and such simple thrills as a savoury olive, who revel in the knowledge reflection on words can bring, who delight in humanity's creative achievements in the past and the present, and who, at the same time, are willing to stand up in unbending opposition to violence, oppression, and abuse of power. The award-winning *Museum of Bone and Water* (*Musée de l'os et de l'eau*) and *Notebook of Roses and Civilization* (*Cahier de roses et de civilisation*) are two of these wonderful collections.

*

In 1985 Brossard expanded her wide-ranging exploration of the traces of virtual universes folded into words and the silences surrounding them through original work with translation. She was herself a translator in French, playing with synonyms and homonyms to reproduce texts using alternative words and phrases so that they are *almost* the same. This amazing virtuosity was demonstrated in *Aviva* (*L'aviva*) and *Mauve Desert* (*Le désert mauve*), where repetition with difference opens welcoming spaces for new, creative readings. During the same period she collaborated with the creative writers Daphne Marlatt and Fred Wah and with translators Barbara Godard and Susanne de Lotbinière-Harwood in translation projects that exhibit the complicity among them in their destabilizing and debauching of received language norms. These translations made her works available to a wide anglophone public. Since that time, Brossard has worked with translators in many languages, and her work has become central to the production of a radical international feminist intertext. Her exuberant joy in creating with words is evident in the traps she sets in her erotically and politically charged love poetry that feminist translators such as Susanne de Lotbinière-Harwood hasten to rise to, as for example in *Sous la langue/Under Tongue*, where sound, meanings, and rhythms are all central to the sense of the work: "Does she frictional

she fluvial she essential does she all along her body love the bite, the sound waves, does she love the state of the world in the blaze of flesh to flesh as seconds flow by silken salty cyprin."[15]

I hope that readers of this selection of Brossard's poetry take full advantage of the enticement to imagine and create that translation offers. For Brossard the notion of the sacrosanct original text is nonsensical. What matters is the endless vertiginous spirals of new words inspired by the words of her or others. Readers are encouraged to peruse the side-by-side texts, to read back and forth between the French and English. The translations are not pale imitations, doomed to be inferior. Instead, they are what Fred Wah called *transcreations* in what he, Lou Nelson, Guy Bennett, Robert Majzels, Erín Moure, and Anne-Marie Wheeler demonstrate in their inspired and complicit texts. As Brossard has said, elusive truths and knowledge lie somewhere in those mysterious white spaces connecting and yet separating the poems on the pages between them. For Brossard, the most important poem is the one readers will write for themselves as they close this volume.

—Louise H. Forsyth

Original French text is provided only for those citations that are not found in the poetry selected for the present volume. Unless otherwise indicated, all translations in this volume are by Louise H. Forsyth: passim and pages 3, 5, 7, 9, 11, 13, 15, 25, 47, 63, 65, 75, 77, 87, 89, 91, 105, 107, 109, 111.

Notes

1 Afterword to Marie-Claire Blais' *A Season in the Life of Emmanuel.*

2 The title of this selection of Brossard's poetry is taken from "Contemporary," in *Installations.*

3 "Notre humanité est dans les lettres et les symboles, notre confort dans les chiffres et les signes," *L'horizon du fragment,* pages 103–4.

4 *Green Night of Labyrinth Park,* page 35. "ce texte, je l'écris à plusieurs niveaux parce que la réalité ne suffit pas, parce que la beauté est exigeante, que les sensations sont multiples, parce que placer dans la langue beaucoup de soi n'élimine pas l'horreur patriarcale, n'explique pas la composition de ma subjectivité et toutes ces images qui bougent comme une femme qui jouit. C'est mobilisée par la matière première du désir que j'écris. La matière des mots [...] éternellement contemporaine de nos joies et corps mobilisés, bruisse, respire, ouvre et suture jusqu'en nos os des puits et des gouffres d'étonnement. J'existe dans la langue écrite parce que c'est là que je décide des pensées qui règlent les questions et les réponses que je donne à la réalité. [La langue] est un terrain fertile en vestiges et vertiges. Dépôt d'illusions,

d'obsessions, de passions, de colère et quoi encore qui nous oblige à transposer la réalité" (*La nuit verte du Parc Labyrinthe*, page 19). This text was inspired by Brossard's participation in the IV International Feminist Book Fair on 24 June 1990 in Barcelona.

5   "Écrire: je suis une femme est plein de conséquences," *L'amèr ou le chapitre effrité*, page 43. *These Our Mothers Or: The Disintegrating Chapter*, page 45.

6   "dans la mystérieuse chorégraphie des mots sur fond de silence que constitue l'espace intérieur," *L'horizon du fragment*, page 47.

7   Title of an influential book of poetry by Paul Chamberland (1964).

8   *La nuit de la poésie* was held on 27 March 1970 at the Théâtre Gesù, in Montreal, and filmed by Jean-Claude Labrecque. The film is currently available for viewing from IMDb.

9   "cette idée de centre blanc, corps zen, corps lumineux qui bientôt sera remplacé par les mots synapses, neurones, cortex exubérant, tout circuit qui donne à rêver," *L'horizon du fragment*, page 115. Brossard created the intriguing image of an "exuberant cortex" in the 1970s to express the excitement of minds newly invigorated and inspired by real contact with their women's bodies and writing their newly recognized realities. "Cortex," used in this way, is a fusion of the two words "corps" and "texte": *corps + texte = cortex*.

10 "Apprendre à flotter entre les mots, les symboles, les nuances et les formes," *L'horizon du fragment*, page 123.

11 In addition to nouns, pronouns, and verbs, Brossard ingeniously uses usually unnoticed parts of speech for poetically subversive ends. For example, she uses the small and seemingly unpresuming word *or* for conjunctive and transitional purposes. It works as a marvellous segue into what is usually a surprising image or elliptical reflection on the senses, sounds, structures, and rhythms of the words in the poem one is reading. By itself the word is commonly used for rhetorical purposes meaning "well then" or "now" in the development of an argument. It produces a quiet pause for breath and thought. At the same time, it echoes in Brossard's texts with its homonym "gold" and also, playing with the kind of paradox of which she is so fond, Brossard may make it suggest the English conjunction "or." Translators have been unable to capture in English the confounding and inspiring flow that *or* can produce. They have frequently left it untranslated, which does not distort meaning but sacrifices poetic magic and polysemia.

12 "Une grammaire ayant pour règle le masculin l'emporte sur le féminin doit être transgressée," *Double impression*, page 43.

13 See "Fragments of a Conversation," page 23.

14 *The Aerial Letter*, page 80. "Les urbaines radicales d'écriture en mouvement changent la réalité qu'elles rappellent au laboratoire de la pensée pour lui faire subir des transformations essentielles à la survie des projets qui nous gardent en vie. Les urbaines radicales traversent les villes et les mythes, y rencontrant toutes sortes de femmes," *La lettre aérienne*, page 58.

15 Fricatelle ruisselle essentielle aime-t-elle le long de son corps la morsure, le bruit des vagues, aime-t-elle l'état du monde dans la flambée des chairs pendant que les secondes s'écoulent cyprine, lutines, marines" (n.p.).

Bibliography

Poetry

Brossard, Nicole. *Aube à la saison* in *Trois*. Montréal: A.G.E.U.M., 1965. 37–68. Reprinted in *Le centre blanc. Poèmes 1965–1975*. Montréal: Éditions de l'Hexagone, Collection « Rétrospectives », 1978. 7–37.

———. *Mordre en sa chair*. Montréal: Éditions Estérel, 1966. Reprinted in *Le centre blanc. Poèmes 1965–1975*. 39–84.

———. *L'écho bouge beau*. Montréal: Éditions Estérel, 1968. Reprinted in *Le centre blanc. Poèmes 1965–1975*. 85–129.

———. *Suite logique*. Montréal: Éditions de l'Hexagone, 1970. Reprinted in *Le centre blanc. Poèmes 1965–1975*. 131–80.

———. *Le centre blanc*. Montréal: Éditions d'Orphée, 1970. Reprinted in *Le centre blanc. Poèmes 1965–1975*. 181–237.

———. *Mécanique jongleuse*. Paris: Génération, 1973. *Mécanique jongleuse*, suivi de *Masculin grammaticale*. Montréal: Éditions de L'Hexagone, 1974. Reprinted in *Le centre blanc. Poèmes 1965–1975*. 239–88. *Daydream Mechanics*, followed by *Masculine Singular*. Trans. Larry Shouldice. Toronto: Coach House Press, 1980.

———. *La partie pour le tout*. Montréal: Éditions de l'Aurore, 1975. Reprinted in *Le centre blanc. Poèmes 1965–1975*. 289–355.

———. *Amantes*. Montréal: Éditions Quinze, 1980. Collection « Réelles ». *Lovhers*. Trans. Barbara Godard. Toronto: Guernica Editions, 1986.

———. "Marginal Way," in *Double impression. Poèmes et textes 1967–1984*. Montréal: Éditions de l'Hexagone, 1984. Collection « Rétrospectives ». 115–20.

———. *L'aviva*. Montréal: Éditions NBJ, 1985.

———, and Daphne Marlatt. *Character/Jeu de lettres*. Montréal: Éditions NBJ, 1986.

———. *Sous la langue/Under Tongue*. Trans. Susanne de Lotbinière-Harwood. Montréal, Charlottetown: L'Essentielle/Gynergy Books, 1987.

———. "Si sismal," in *À tout regard*. Montréal: Éditions NBJ / Bibliothèque québécoise, 1989. 121–28. "If Yes Seismal." Transcreated by Fred Wah. *Absinthe* 5.1 (Summer 1992).

———. *Installations (avec et sans pronoms)*. Trois-Rivières / Paris: Écrits des Forges / Castor Astral, 1989. *Installations (with and without pronouns)*. Trans. Erín Moure and Robert Majzels. Winnipeg: Muses' Company, 2000.

———. *Langues obscures*. Montréal: Éditions de l'Hexagone, 1992.

———. *La nuit verte du Parc Labyrinthe / Green Night of Labyrinth Park / La Noche verde del Parque Laberinto*. Trans. Lou Nelson and Marina Fe. Laval: Éditions Trois, 1992.

————. *Typhon dru*. London: Reality Street Editions, 1997. Bilingual ed. Trans. Caroline Bergvall. French text previously published in two limited editions, 1989, 1990.

————. *Vertige de l'avant-scène*. Trois-Rivières: Écrits des Forges, 1997.

————. *Au présent des veines*. Trois-Rivières / Luxembourg / La Réunion: Écrits des Forges / Éditions Phi / Grand Océan, 1999.

————. *La matière heureuse manoeuvre encore* in *Au présent des veines*. Trois-Rivières / Luxembourg / La Réunion: Écrits des Forges / Éditions Phi / Grand Océan, 1999. 103–14. *Harmonious Matter Is Still Manoeuvring*. Trans. Louise H. Forsyth, in "Bursting Boundaries in the Vast Complication of Beauty: Transported by Nicole Brossard's *Au présent des veines*." *Verdure* 5–6 (February 2002).

————. *Musée de l'os et de l'eau*. Saint-Hippolyte: Éditions du Noroît, 1999/2008. *Museum of Bone and Water*. Trans. Robert Majzels and Erín Moure. Toronto: House of Anansi Press, 2003.

————. *Je m'en vais à Trieste*. Trois-Rivières / Luxembourg / Limoges: Écrits des Forges / Éditions Phi / Le bruit des autres, 2003.

————. *Cahier de roses et de civilisation*. *Écritures 2*. Trois-Rivières: Éditions d'Art Le Sabord, 2003. Gravures de Francine Simonin. *Notebook of Roses and Civilization*. Trans. Robert Majzels and Erín Moure. Toronto: Coach House Books, 2007.

————. *Après les mots*. Trois-Rivières / Luxembourg: Écrits des Forges / Éditions Phi, 2007.

————. *Ardeur*. Luxembourg / Trois-Rivières: Editions Phi / Ecrits des Forges, 2008.

————. *Shadow: Soft et Soif*, in *Ardeur*. Luxembourg / Trois-Rivières: Éditions Phi / Écrits des Forges, 2008. 77–111. *Shadow: Soft et Soif*. Trans. Guy Bennett. Los Angeles: Seeing Eye Books, 2003.

————. *D'aube et de civilisation*. *Anthologie: poèmes de Nicole Brossard 1965–2007*. Ed. Louise Dupré. Montréal: Éditions Typo, 2008.

————. *L'aviva/Aviva*. Trans. Anne-Marie Wheeler. Bilingual edition. Vancouver: Nomades Press, 2008.

Prose

Brossard, Nicole. *Un livre*. Montréal: Éditions du Jour, 1970. *A Book*. Trans. Larry Shouldice. Toronto: Coach House Quebec Translations, 1976.

————. "Vaseline." *La Barre du Jour* 42 (automne 1973), reprinted in *Double impression*. *Poèmes et textes 1967–1984*. Montréal: Éditions L'Hexagone, 1984. 39–47.

———. *Sold-out. Étreinte / illustration.* Montréal: Éditions du Jour, 1973. *Turn of a Pang.* Trans. Patricia Claxton. Toronto: Coach House Quebec Translations, 1976.

———. *French Kiss. Étreinte-exploration.* Montréal: Éditions du Jour, 1974. *French Kiss or: A Pang's Progress.* Trans. Patricia Claxton. Toronto: Coach House Quebec Translations, 1986.

———. "*E* muet mutant." *La Barre du Jour* 50 (hiver 1975), reprinted in *Double impression. Poèmes et textes 1967–1984.* Montréal: Éditions de l'Hexagone, 1984. 51–70.

———. "L'écrivain." *La nef des sorcières.* Montréal: Éditions Quinze, 1976. 73–80. "The Writer." *A Clash of Symbols* in *Anthology of Québec Women's Plays in English Translation. Vol. I (1966–1986).* Ed. Louise H. Forsyth. Toronto: Playwrights Press Canada, 2006. Trans. Linda Gaboriau. 325–29.

———. *L'amèr ou le chapitre effrité.* Montréal: Éditions Quinze, 1977. *These Our Mothers Or: The Disintegrating Chapter.* Trans. Barbara Godard. Toronto: Coach House Quebec Translations, 1983.

———. *Le sens apparent.* Paris: Flammarion, 1980. *Surfaces of Sense.* Trans. Fiona Strachan. Toronto: Coach House Quebec Translations, 1989.

———. *Picture Theory.* Montréal: Éditions Nouvelle Optique, 1982. *Picture Theory.* Trans. Barbara Godard. Toronto: Guernica Editions, 1991.

———. *Journal intime ou Voilà donc un manuscrit.* Montréal: Éditions Les Herbes Rouges, 1984. *Intimate Journal or Here's a Manuscript.* Trans. Barbara Godard. Toronto: Mercury Press, 2004.

———. *La lettre aérienne.* Montréal: Éditions du Remue-ménage, 1985. *The Aerial Letter.* Trans. Marlene Wildeman. Toronto: Women's Press, 1988.

———. *Le désert mauve.* Montréal: Éditions de l'Hexagone, 1987. *Mauve Desert.* Trans. Susanne de Lotbinière-Harwood. Toronto: Coach House Press, 1990.

———. "Poetic Politics," in *The Politics of Poetic Form. Poetry and Public Policy,* ed. Charles Bernstein. New York: Roof, 1990. 107–26. Republished in *Fluid Arguments: Essays,* ed. Susan Rudy. Toronto: Mercury Press, 2005. 26–36.

———. "Afterword," in Marie-Claire Blais, *A Season in the Life of Emmanuel.* Trans. Derek Coltman. *Une saison dans la vie d'Emmanuel.* Toronto: McClelland & Stewart, 1992.

———. *Baroque d'aube.* Montréal: Éditions de l'Hexagone, 1995. *Baroque at Dawn.* Trans. Patricia Claxton. Toronto: McClelland & Stewart, 1997.

———. *Elle serait la première phrase de mon prochain roman. She Would Be the First Sentence of My Next Novel.* Trans. Susanne de Lotbinière-Harwood. Toronto: Mercury Press, 1998.

———. *L'horizon du fragment.* Paroisse Notre-Dame-des-Neiges: Éditions Trois-Pistoles, 2004.

————. *Hier*. Montréal: Québec/Amérique, 2001. *Yesterday, at the Hotel Clarendon*. Trans. Susanne de Lotbinière-Harwood. Toronto: Coach House Books, 2005.

————. *Fluid Arguments: Essays Written in French and English*. Ed. Susan Rudy. Toronto: Mercury Press, 2005.

————. "Fragments of a Conversation," in *Nicole Brossard: Essays on Her Work*, ed. Louise H. Forsyth. Toronto: Guernica Editions, 2006. 19–33.

————. *La capture du sombre*. Montréal: Leméac, 2007. *Fences in Breathing*. Trans. Susanne de Lotbinière-Harwood. Toronto: Coach House Books, 2009.

Anthologies

Brossard, Nicole, ed. *Les stratégies du réel. The Story So Far 6*. Montréal / Toronto: La Nouvelle Barre du Jour / Coach House Press, 1979.

Brossard, Nicole, and Lisette Girouard, eds. *Anthologie de la poésie des femmes au Québec*. Montréal: Éditions du Remue-ménage, 1991. 2nd ed.: *Anthologie de la poésie des femmes au Québec des origines à nos jours*. Montréal: Éditions du Remue-ménage, 2003.

Brossard, Nicole, ed. *Poèmes à dire la francophonie. 38 poètes contemporains*. Bordeaux: CNDP / Castor Astral, 2002.

Brossard, Nicole, ed. *Baiser vertige. Prose et poésie gaies et lesbiennes au Québec*. Montréal: Éditions Typo, 2006.

Recent Publications on the Works of Nicole Brossard

Forsyth, Louise, ed. *Nicole Brossard: Essays on Her Works*. Toronto: Guernica Editions, 2006.

Lundgren, Jodi, and Kelly-Anne Maddox, eds. "Revisiting Nicole Brossard: Québécois Feminist Subjectivity in the 21st Century." *HOW* 2 2.3 (Spring 2005). http://www.asu.edu/pipercwcenter/how2journal/.

Russo, Linda, and Anna Reckin, eds. "Nicole Brossard Special Feature." *Verdure* 5–6 (February 2002): 28–143.

Sur fil de lumière
je suspends la poésie
comme guirlandes

orbite de mes horizons
je gravis ses enceintes
glissant sur l'archipel
de rivières démentes

j'ai la poésie plantée au ventre et au coeur
éboulis qui m'invente des paysages
je m'ouvre comme une huître sous le couteau
de son arc-en-ciel

étang de mes étoiles qui foisonne
le vase de la solitude
bouée de ma réalité
algue de mes abandons

je m'ancre à ton corail

On strands of light
I am hanging poetry
like garlands

orbit my horizons
I ascend its enclosures
slipping on the archipelago
of raging rivers

planted in my belly and my heart poetry is
scree inventing landscapes for me
I open myself like an oyster under the knife
of its rainbow

lagoon of my swarming stars
vessel of solitude
buoy of reality
alga of my abandons

I anchor myself on your coral

La loi du muscle

il est certain qu'elle est quelque part
    entre le silence et le cri
et que son geste repose sur l'effort et la caresse

vous et moi tout en sueur
    de sentir la loi du muscle
au noeud serré des rigueurs de la vie

j'anime le bois qui s'allonge en moi
    l'heureuse sève
la sentence du muscle devant la solitude

et rien ne persiste contre cette audace

ce temps de chair
réveille jusqu'à mon dos la démarche du coeur
bouche en lamelles de sursaut
je sers au muscle l'océan de ma prunelle
la vraie chaleur des tropiques
qui ne s'échange contre rien
si ce n'est la rafale et toute sensation

la loi du muscle porte cicatrice
à même la nourriture de nos ventres
jusqu'à la sphère des parfaites ivresses
et je dépose à la faille de sa planète
tout le sang qui répond à moi-même

que je partage à vos lèvres
la ride de mon front

ainsi le jour sera vaincu
    comme la nuit
sans que le souffle faiblisse en ma poitrine

et nous boirons la grisaille des étoiles
    en pleine veine
    en bordure du bras
à tout ce qui naît d'image et de couleur

Muscle's Law

for sure it is somewhere
      between silence and shout
and her gestures spring from effort and caress

you and I all in a sweat
      from feeling muscle's law
within its knot tight from life's hardships

I bring the wood stretching out in me to life
      vital sap
muscle's sentence facing solitude

and nothing can resist this audacity

this time of flesh
makes my heart's move shiver down my back
mouth in sparkling streamers
I offer to muscle the ocean of my eye's pupil
true heat of the tropics
that nothing can replace
squall and full sensation

muscle's law shows scars
there where our bellies are fed
out to the sphere of perfect exhilarations
and I place on its planet's fault line
my full blood response

may I share on your lips
the wrinkle of my brow

thus the day will be vanquished
      like the night
breath unfailing in my breast

and we'll drink the greyness of the stars
      blood racing
        alongside the arm
to all that is born from image and from colour

neutre le monde m'enveloppe neutre
avec des éclairs de contradiction
cela est nu désolé et aspire quand même
je le sais au rythme qui s'apprête là

neutral the world envelops me neutral
with flashes of contradiction
this is bare desolate and yet draws me in
I can tell by the rhythm preparing there

écoute plutôt paisiblement l'écorce craquer
l'écorce toi imbibée d'huile ou de savon
ongles dents crâne murmurer leur
écho coûte que coûte
                    l'ombre sonore t'envahir

listen quite peacefully the crust cracking
the crust imbued with oil or with soap you
nails teeth skull murmuring their
echo cost what may

        the sonorous shadow invading you

en ces temps opaques le ciel remorquait tant de délires

or l'artifice scintille et s'expose
éventuel accomplissement
tout en surface
d'émeute en fabuleuses suites sonores
ledit rapport rature
double exaspération
le code pavane
le code analyse le code dicte
et tout à l'opposé voici paraître le code tendre

This is a slightly modified version of the poem which appeared in the 1970
publication of *Suite logique* This version appeared in *D'aube et de civilisation* (page
66), edited by Louise Dupré.

in those opaque times the sky was trailing so much delirium

now artifice shimmers and exposes itself
eventual achievement
right on surface
from riot to fabulous sonorous suites
the declared relation rips
double exasperation
the code struts
the code analyses the code dictates
and on the opposite side here comes the tender code

entre code et code l'espace est illusoire
point de lieu propre à la dénonciation
la terminologie modifie

le code s'infiltre
la moindre tentative finit par rompre

désormais le sens en a deux
un de trop
l'artifice est inévitable

voilà comment

between code and code space is illusory
no place suitable for denunciation
terminology modifies

code filters in
the slightest attempt breaks down in the end

henceforth sense has two
one too many
artifice is inevitable

that's how

suspension de l'acte
comprendre est un séjour
excluant toute définition

respirer ne rien manifester
alors que tout s'engouffre dans

visage perpétuel
peu importe le masque
sexe perpétuel

action suspended
understanding is a haven
excluding all definition

breathing revealing nothing
while everything tumbles in

perpetual face
mask matter little
perpetual sex

IV.

le mot vertige puis situé entre le voyant et le
mot le mot à nouveau dans un ensemble où
l'abstrait prend tout des désirs devient forme
vie m'absorbe les mots tombent mais qualifier
n'est pas la solution l'unité est hors la ligne
continue dans le point final qui s'éloigne
toujours se soustrait au geste ultime qui
déposerait tout en même temps et lieu sous la
forme d'un point blanc en l'espace blanc

IV.

the word vertigo placed then between the
seer and the word the word again in general
when abstraction takes everything from
desires becomes form life absorbs me words
fail but specifying is not the solution unity
is outside the line continues in the period
that distances itself always withdraws in the
ultimate gesture that will set everything down
in the same time place in the form of a white
mark in a blank space

Translated by Barbara Godard

V.

attentive au silence à l'instant où rien ne se
passe où le vide se fait la vie en place tout
du corps s'affranchit de la vie l'extase la vie
du centre état pure vigilance quand tout de
l'esprit existe sans contrainte continuel état
de veille qui se perpétue de sourire en
sourire à l'intérieur de la même attentive et
heureuse personne personne là

V.

attentive to the silence to the moment when
nothing happens when the blank becomes
life in its place the whole body is freed from
life ecstasy the life of the centre state pure
vigilance when the whole mind exists
without constraint continual state of
watching established from smile to smile
inside the same attentive and happy
person's body nobody there

Translated by Barbara Godard

son désir l'explore
yeux et conséquence de la circonstance
son regard l'infiltre plus parfaitement
que les déserts lisses et mouvants
(termes d'agitation: la mécanique
souterraine
l'ensemble des crues et des hauts cris)
son désir
sur le masculin grammaticale
ramification des doigts malines

her desire explores her
eyes and consequence of the circumstance
her look seeps into her more perfectly
than the smooth and restless deserts
(terms of movement: subterranean
mechanism
the combination of floods and loud cries)
her desire
in the masculine singular
branching out of lacy fingers

verte vague sur le ventre sur l'échine
fauche et frôle et somme le sexe d'
entame le souffle
sur-le-champ tout le parcours
jusqu'en la poitrine vague
flottante

la conséquence d'essouff d's
l'x du exe l'axe de plaisir
force la forme et le poids de l'ongle
sur l'épine de chair qui convient
sur la peau pour
un renversement d'allures vives vers
les herbes   y rouler d'inclinaison

green billows on the belly on the spine
reap and rub and overwhelm the sex of
bring breathing to
there and then the whole course
right to the vague floating
breast

result of getting short of brea   th's
the x of ex   axis of pleasure
force the form and the weight of   finger
nail on the spine of flesh appropriate
on the skin for
a reversal of brisk gaits to
the grasses   rolling in them leaningly

Body imagery

je prends la page par le côté incertain presque
désespérant de quiconque sent sa folie sourdre
dompteuse arrogante et surtout jamais rassasiée, à
l'écoute de toutes les célébrations. la folie fertile qui se
lamente et explore dedans la source vive des séjours
intérieurs. et toujours je pense à toi comme ma plus
belle et vulnérable certitude

I dive into the page through the uncertain side almost despairing as one would feel the outburst of her madness aggressive arrogant above all never satiated hearkening to all celebrations. fertile madness that laments and explores within herself living source of inner havens. and always you are on my mind woman of my most beautiful and vulnerable certainties

Le corps des mères enlacées, en réalité, c'est aussi le mien trouble et captivée par cette hérédité qui se forme intérieure tâche d'eau, l'algue frôlant le cil. Ma forme n'est plus intacte enlacée avec son corps, mais comme une structure parée à la jouissance. Publiquement la fiction publiquement les frasques, les fresques, multiples dans le prisme, cavalièrement publiques les filles mères et fantastiques allongeant leurs bras comme des interventions sexuelles dans les pages politiques du quotidien. Le corps des mères enlacées, en réalité, c'est une bien belle expression.

The bodies of mothers entwined, in reality, it is also mine uneasy and enraptured by this heredity which takes shape inside the water drop, seaweed brushing eyelash. My form is no longer intact entwined with her body, but like a structure adorned for sexual bliss. Publicly fiction, publicly escapades, frescoes, multiple in the prism, the daughters mothers cavalierly public and fantastic stretching out their arms like sexual intercessions in the political pages of the daily paper. The bodies of mothers entwined, in reality, is a truly beautiful expression.

(4): Amantes / écrire

quelque part toujours un énoncé, la peau
concentrée
à l'inverse du système
attentive aux circonstances amoureuses, ce
texte
à l'oeil: juin suscité par l'audace
lèvres précises ou cet attrait du clitoris
sa pensée inédite qui rend au corps son
intelligence
car   chaque tremblement vise l'émergence
juin la fièvre la fin des couples
leur prolongement comme le plus inattendu des
silences: amoureuses

la texture des identités

---

en réalité, il n'y a pas de fiction

(4): Lovhers / Write

somewhere always a statement, skin
concentrated
system inverted
attentive to the phases of love, this text
under the eye: June aroused by audacity
precise lips or this allurement of the clitoris
its unrecorded thought giving the body back
intelligence
because each shiver aims at the emergence
June the fever the end of couples
their prolongation like the most unexpected of
silences: lesbian lovhers

the texture of identities

_____

in reality, there is no fiction

selon les années de la réalité, imaginer les
parcours de ville en ville pour parler les
versions lisses qui se glissent en chaque corps
suscitant le déploiement, l'excitation: partout
des femmes faisaient le guet de la seule
manière plausible: belles et graves dans leur
énergie de spirale en spirale

— sous les oranges de L.A. la frontière de feu
entre le palmier dérisoire et les fleurs rouges
comme un papier d'argent. j'assiste au
croisement accessible de tous les dangers qui
survoltent les peaux compatibles   l'excitation:
ce qui met la réalité en péril, comme une
invitation à la connaissance, présence intégrale

— près de moi, sa pensée fluide, l'encre,
à peine sa voix cherchant les mots
à quelques pieds de distance, nos actes de
recueillement face à l'écrit
tendue vers elle de la même intensité
que penchée sur elle: souffle

JE N'ARRÊTE PAS DE LIRE

according to the years of reality, imagine going
from city to city to recite the smooth versions that
slip into each body instigating the unfolding, the
excitation: everywhere women kept watch in the
only way plausible: beautiful and serious in their
energy from spiral to spiral

— under the oranges of L.A. the frontier of fire
between the ludicrous palm tree and the red
flowers like aluminum foil. i am present at the
accessible intersection of all the dangers which
boost the current of compatible skins excitation:
what imperils reality, like an invitation to
knowledge, integral presence

— near me, her fluid thought, ink,
her voice faintly seeking out words
a few feet away, our acts of
meditation face to face with writing
stretched out towards her with the same intensity
as my bending over her: breath

I DON'T STOP READING / DELIRING

« la splendeur » dit O.

« your strong tongue and slender fingers
reaching where I had been waiting years for you
in my rose-wet cave — whatever happens, this is. »
Adrienne Rich

---

partout le projet des villes et des géographies pour
inciter nos corps à toujours plus de fluidité, chute
inlassable
dans nos bouches des saveurs rendent cette
approche du délire compatible avec l'esprit et
nous imaginons de nouvelles moeurs avec ces
bouches mêmes qui savent tenir un discours, les
nôtres au goût des mots au goût du baiser (je
n'arrête pas de lire — excitation: ce qui me suscite
inédite dans ma peau)

"the splendour," says O.

"your strong tongue and slender fingers
reaching where I had been waiting years for you
in my rose-wet cave — whatever happens, this is."
Adrienne Rich

---

everywhere the project of cities and geographies
to arouse our bodies to ever greater fluidity,
endless flood into our mouths of savours makes
this approach of delirium compatible with the
mind and we imagine new customs with these
same mouths that know how to make a speech,
ours tasting of words tasting of kisses (i don't stop
reading / deliring — excitation: what arouses the
unrecorded in my skin)

« la science » dit Xa.

« lécher jusqu'au coeur notre vaste complot »
Louky Bersianik

---

dans la posture heureuse des mains sur la hanche
une tendresse sexuelle parcourt toutes les
distances urbaines — on n'y voit que du feu, la
permanence du désir dans nos exercices de
précision car nos lèvres chercheuses captent toute
notre attention, convoquées par la science de nos
musiques

juin, l'urgence du repli: couple ramifié tenant
dans ma main un livre de Djuna Barnes, je
n'arrête pas de lire, j'ai besoin de toutes mes
tensions face à la dérive car dans tous mes
muscles, un besoin de souplesse, c'est alors que je
fais la spirale devant toi et que la plus étrange
séduction prend forme en même temps que
l'étreinte.   on dirait ce soir que la nuit
nous pousse à des comportements de douce
avidité et que nos bouches s'éteignent lentement,
on ne peut plus attentives à leurs effets.

"science" says Xa.

"lick to the heart of our vast plot"
                              Louky Bersianik

---

in the happy position of hands on hips a sexual
tenderness runs throughout distances — fire is all
we can see, the permanence of desire in our
precision exercises because our searching lips
captivate all our attention, called forth by the
science of our music

June, the urgency of the fold: ramified couple
holding in my hand a book by Djuna Barnes, I
can't stop reading / deliring, i need all my tensions
when confronting the drift because in all my
muscles, a need for suppleness, that is when i
make a spiral in front of you and when the
strangest seduction takes form at the same time as
the embrace.   tonight it seems night pushes us to
behaviour which is sweetly desiring and our
mouths are slowly extinguished, we can't be more
attentive to their effects.

MA continent

MA *continent* qui possède à cette heure
toutes mes salives, car chez toi, j'ai
oublié le texte que je voulais sous tes
yeux de lecture qui ont vu passer des
siècles de fantasmes, de peau, le bruit/
la détonation. (ma) c'est un espace/
une hypothèse

MY Continent

MY *continent* she now has
all my saliva, since, at your place, i've
forgotten the text i wanted before your
reading eyes which have watched centuries
of hallucinations, of skin, pass, the noise/
detonation. (mâ)* it's a space / an hypothesis

---

* mâ — Japanese term for space
 ma — possessive pronoun, feminine gender, in French (Barbara Godard)

ma continent femme de tous les espaces
cortex et flot: un sens de la gravité
qui *me met au monde*
ma différente matière à existence qui
comble et évacue cette tension *unique*
qui ressemble à l'ultime vitalité et
sagesse où intelligence et seins, cuisses
successivement dormantes et d'agitation
les poitrines ont la raison du souffle
que nous y trouvons / écriture

my continent woman of all the spaces
cortex and flood: a sense of gravity
bringing me into the world
my different matter into existence which
fills and drains this *singular* tension
like the ultimate vitality and
wisdom where intelligence and breasts, thighs
one after the other sleeping and agitation
breasts get the better of breath
we find there / writing

ma continent des espaces de raison et
(d'amour) comme une histoire spatiale
où nous pouvons dire dans le concret
des allégeances et des caresses en silence
une forme de réverbération / je traverse
les villes sans simuler *la nature* car
je suis si civilisée face à la mer
au comble de l'eau, persistante / j'ai lu
« Toute la mer va vers la ville »
et aussi dans ta langue
« Non smettete di delirare, questo è il
momento de l'utopia »

my continent of spaces of reason and
(of love) like a history of space
where we can speak concretely
about allegiance and caresses in silence
a form of reverberation / i cut across
cities without simulating *nature* because
i'm so civilized before the sea
at flood tide, persistent / i read
"The whole sea goes toward the city"
and also in your language
"Non smettete di delirare, questo è il
momento de l'utopia"

ma continent multiple de celles qui ont signé:
Djuna Barnes, Jane Bowles, Gertrude Stein,
Natalie Barney, Michèle Causse, Marie-Claire
Blais, Jovette Marchessault, Adrienne Rich,
Mary Daly, Colette et Virginia, les autres
noyées, Cristina Peri Rossi, Louky Bersianik,
Pol Pelletier, Maryvonne si attentive, Monique
Wittig, Sande Zeig, Anna d'Argentine, Kate
Millett, Jeanne d'Arc Jutras, Marie Lafleur,
Jane Rule, Renée Vivien, Romaine Brooks,
écrire: le réel / la peau clairvoyante
prunelle essentielle dans le déploiement
de ma conscience et *expression*: mon double
une singulière mobilité et le continent
certes une joie

my continent multiplied by those who have
signed: Djuna Barnes, Jane Bowles, Gertrude
Stein, Natalie Barney, Michèle Causse, Marie-
Claire Blais, Jovette Marchessault, Adrienne
Rich, Mary Daly, Colette and Virginia, the other
drowned ones, Cristina Peri Rossi, Louky
Bersianik, Pol Pelletier, Maryvonne so attentive,
Monique Wittig, Sande Zeig, Anna d'Argentine,
Kate Millett, Jeanne d'Arc Jutras, Marie Lafleur,
Jane Rule, Renée Vivien, Romaine Brooks
to write: the real / the skin clairvoyant
pupil essential in the unfolding
of my consciousness and *expression*: my double
a singular mobility and the continent
indeed a joy

ma continent, je veux parler l'effet
radical de la lumière au grand jour
aujourd'hui, je t'ai serrée de près,
aimée de toute civilisation, de toute
texture, de toute géométrie et de braise,
délirantes, comme on écrit: et
mon corps est ravi

my continent, i mean to talk about the radical
effect of light in broad daylight
today, i've held you close,
loved by every civilization, every
texture, every geometry and ember,
delirious, as it is written: and
my body is enraptured

Marginal Way

l'intention la beauté extrême
le paysage tu l'ajoutes à la lumière
du penchant
l'heure est plausible *beyond reality*
le corps cosmique s'approche au loin
in the marginal way, l'attitude flagrante

*

ce n'est pas familier dans l'ombre
la falaise
les frontières abîment le regard
pourtant l'être je dis franchir l'écho
aérienne dans l'équation au-dessus
des mers, c'est syllabe ici l'espoir
my mind agite l'essentielle

*

si dans l'ombre je pense à la passion
au dos des fragments en toute quiétude
c'est un aspect de la lecture
une position prise pour y voir
la matière aux frontières fend les yeux
j'existe en direct

Marginal Way

intention extreme beauty
landscape you add it to the light
of the penchant
the hour is propitious *beyond reality*
the cosmic body approaches far off
in the marginal way, flagrant attitude

*

it's not familiar in shadow
the cliff
boundaries destroy sight
yet being I say traverse the echo
aerial feminine in the equation above
the seas, syllable here hope
my mind stirs woman essential

*

if in shadow I think of passion
on the back of fragments in full quietude
it's an aspect of reading
a position taken to see there
matter on boundaries cleaves eyes
I exist live to air

l'émotion est un signe
une réplique attentive au sens

l'aviva

l'aviva son visage et les relais
de connivence l'ampleur des images
toute penchée sur l'attrait, sa bouche
or les lèvres il y a normalement mots
au bord de l'émoi une phrase reliée
tapie et à l'insu caressée
tout en longeant les bras d'excitation
s'appliquer, l'idée tenait tenace
car lier

l'en suite traduite

l'anima l'image et les effets
d'alliance teneur du visage
toute pensée sur les traits se couche
or les livres singulièrement toi d'aloi
au loin l'émoi qui s'écrie
à l'infinie d'utopie l'ainsi caresse
d'excitation longe le geste au comble
langue sujet vorace s'appliquer ignée
ç'allier

emotion is a sign
a sense-attentive reply

aviva

aviva a face and the relaying
of complicity, ample images
leaning toward the lure, her mouth
now the looks there are normally words
on the edge of emotion a phrase related
hidden and unknowingly caressed
while running the length of her arms in excitation
applied, the idea tenable tenacious
for linking

the latest translated

anima image and effects
of affinity facial formation
all learning on her traits laid down
now the books singularly, you: virtue
in the distance, emotion emotes
in the infinite utopia thus caress
in excitation running the height of the gesture
tongue voracious subject applied igneous
liaising

Translated by Anne-Marie Wheeler

l'aviva

car l'aviva, l'attisa lève le voile
sur la conscience immédiatement
d'un toucher et d'une proposition
qui vive au fond du cerveau
précipite les images et une passion
qui savait retenir dans la mémoire
le luire de jouir virage des hanches

l'en suite traduite

car voilà que lèvres encore d'elle
la science exactement l'immédiat
des sens avouer l'intention
qui mire au fond la peau
c'est récite la version la page
elle se souvenait et trop frémir
au large des sens la coïncidence

aviva

for the aviva, stirred her lifts the veil
on consciousness immediately
a touch and a proposition
alive deep in the brain
precipitates images and a passion
who knew to hold in memory
the glistening coming swaying of hips

the latest translated

for here that lips still hers
the science exactly the immediacy
of senses to avow intent
that mirrors the depths of skin
it's recite the version the page
she remembered and too to shudder
at large from sense coincidence

Translated by Anne-Marie Wheeler

Si sismal

si aboyer ou noyer la voix
parmi les images et les mots
éveille un peu de crainte
abrite alors la figure choisie
le bord renversé de vivre
labelle spacieux

si quelque tissu de soie persiste
sur les lèvres et trop excite
respire d'un air naturel
même si demain va vite
dans l'anatomie
cherche d'autres récits

si à petits coups de langue
d'expression la tension continue
rapproche les mots crus
l'horizon s'il le faut
jusqu'en la bouche

si le timbre de la voix
se transforme et que trop de chaos
ou que mélancolie s'installe
combine la variété des réponses
la théâtralité de parler

si ça recommence et qu'il fait chaud
trop chaud encore dans les jointures
appuie partout sur le quotidien
il reste de grands trous
des saveurs inexplicables
baies, corail, littorines

si, tu trembles, tu vois bien
forcément il y a du blanc
c'est vrai et forcément
tu trembles

If Yes Seismal

if above the clysmic bark heaves
noise the voice detonates images and
words for life a little crazy we
think but all right before the actual
figures choose choice the border
labels space in you

if any persistent tissue bristles pitapat
on the heart's much too excited lip
could be the air's too rare
naturally some same body
remembers too late
to search for another wave

if a small cup of language
soups intention with a continued
expression against word crust
until the horizon of approach
whose fault whose lips

if the forest of the voice
transforms into the trop of chaos
or melancholy installs itself
in the parlour of surprise plant
variety re-speak pond

if the see-saw bounces back hot to trot
trembling shows up again late cell
synapse applied part out on
a day of rest great truth
a vague smack of the lips
gulfs, coral, littoral

if, you tremble, you should see
inevitably there is some white
it is true and of course
you tremble

Transcreation by Fred Wah

Réalité

la réalité est une petite craie
qui trace sans tracer
la vie, son déchiffrement
dans le bleu l'ombre des récits
la réalité existe ailleurs toujours
ailleurs
à la ferveur du corps la langue souligne
l'appétit de vivre au milieu
la réalité je la compare pour décrire
le trajet sournois, la luxuriance
de la fiction dans une vie

Reality

reality is a bit of chalk
traces without tracing
life, its deciphering
in blue the shadow of narratives
reality always exists
elsewhere
with the body's fervour the tongue stresses
the appetite for living in the midst
reality I compare it to describe
the sly trajectory, luxuriance
of fiction in a life

Langue

parce que c'est avec la bouche
la parole est un manège maximal
autour du ventre
un flux de tendresse et de peur
qui donne au verbe être sa démesure
recto verso la parole lèche tout

Tongue

because it is with the mouth
speech is an ultimate machination
around the belly
a flux of tenderness and fear
that makes unfathomable the verb to be
recto verso speech licks all

Installation

chaque matin je m'intéresse à la vie
de grands détours et des preuves
au cœur de la langue des pans de siècle
icônes, soies, souvent manuscrits
le corps impair des femmes
les grands séismes
de loin ça se voit
je m'installe dans mon corps
de manière à pouvoir bouger
quand une femme me fait signe

Installation

every morning I take an interest in life
huge detours and proofs
the tail ends of century at the heart of language
icons, silks, often manuscripts
the odd-numbered body of women
great quakes
visible from afar
I settle into my body's installation
so as to be able to respond
when a woman gives me a sign

Contemporaine

là où ça fait mal dans la vie
par touches successives
ce n'est pas la mort
mais la mobilité de la lumière
le don que nous avons d'aggraver la beauté

Contemporary

where it hurts in life
by successive strokes
it's not death
but mobility of light
our gift for aggravating beauty

Je m'intéresse à la connaissance parce qu'il y a des structures invisibles dans nos os pour nous sortir de l'enfance et des manœuvres familiales. L'enfance ne suffit pas quand on vit au milieu des planètes et du mensonge. Certes, le chien de l'âme, perché sur son anatomie, grand interprète des langues obscures, veille pour ne pas compromettre nos chances de salut au milieu des êtres parlants, dispense toujours un peu d'espoir à force de ressembler à quelqu'un. Je suppose que le recours collectif au *je* facilite l'intensité au milieu des planètes et du mensonge.

I indulge in knowledge because there are invisible structures in our bones to get us out of childhood and family manoeuvres. Childhood does not suffice when one lives surrounded by planets and lies. Certainly, *le chien de l'âme,* perched on its anatomy, grand interpreter of obscure tongues, keeps watch to make sure our chances at salvation are not compromised among speaking beings, always dispenses a bit of hope by virtue of its resemblance to someone. I suppose that collective recourse to the *I* makes intensity easier in the midst of planets and lies.

Je m'intéresse à la connaissance parce que je
voudrais de l'univers soigner le sens autour
d'une femme et de plusieurs. Oui, c'est rap-
proché de la parole d'honneur que le désir peut
rendre dicible la comparaison que nous fai-
sons entre la mer et nos intentions de bonheur.
Je m'intéresse à la connaissance parce que
trop de vie nous échappe lorsque nous exer-
çons notre faculté de joie

I indulge in knowledge because I would like to nurture the sense in the universe surrounding one and several women. Yes, it's close to the word of honour that desire can find words for the comparison that we draw between the sea and our intentions for happiness. I indulge in knowledge because too much of life eludes us when we exercise our capacity for joy.

SEPTIÈME TOURNANT *entre l'histoire bordée de visions*

cela fait maintenant plus de deux heures que je circule dans le labyrinthe. Il me semble être passée au même endroit plusieurs fois mais je n'en suis plus certaine. Chaque tournant ressemble à un autre. Tous très verts comme la nuit. Brise, odeurs justes, silence vertical. Épaules qui longent la nuit comme un absolu *in the never ending process of hope*. Je ne sais plus si je cherche le centre ou la sortie, je sais seulement qu'entre les beaux arbustes du jardin *del laberinto*, j'aperçois au loin les premiers bateaux français qui remontèrent le fleuve Saint-Laurent. Je les vois frôlant les baleines et l'horizon, je les vois sur la rive décharger, entre les vivres, les armes et les outils, une langue française qui bientôt servira à décrire les aurores boréales, le vent du Nord et le silence vertical des rives enneigées. Cela fait longtemps. Mes yeux ne savent plus dans quelle direction aller, du côté du fleuve, au rythme des vagues, du côté de la nuit *solo mujeres*, au rythme des corps dansant. Mes yeux cherchent les grands sourcils noirs de Frida Khalo, les yeux perçants de Gertrude, le corps flottant de Virginia. Puis les bateaux revinrent, cette fois-ci remplis de rondeaux, sonnets, madrigaux, odes, fabliaux et parodies qui résistèrent aux neiges successives. Me voici maintenant entourée de baleines et d'orignaux, au milieu des goélands, entrée dans le tourment des formes, en nage soudain du désir qui monte en moi de voir entre mes lèvres, ma langue glisser sur la chair très tendre du mot clitoris. *Breathe your silence, respira en tu memoria*, féconde la rhétorique. Je taille dans l'histoire et le présent la subjectivité de celle qui me ressemble avec sa bouche.

SEVENTH BEND *between history framed in visions*

I have been walking in the labyrinth for more than two hours now. I think I have passed the same place several times, but I am no longer sure. Each bend resembles another. All as green as the night. Breeze, hints of fragrance, vertical silence. Shoulders that rub up against the night like an absolute *in the never ending process of hope*. I no longer know if I seek the centre or the exit, I know only that in the distance, between the beautiful bushes of the jardin *del laberinto*, I see the first French ships that sailed up the St. Lawrence River. I watch them brush against the whales and the horizon, I see them on the shore, unloading — in the midst of provisions, weapons and tools — a French language that will soon be used to describe the aurora borealis, the North wind and the vertical silence of snowy shores. That was a long time ago. My eyes no longer know where to look, to the river and the rhythm of the waves, or to the *solo mujeres* night and the rhythm of dancing bodies. My eyes seek the long black eyebrows of Frida Kahlo, the piercing eyes of Gertrude, the floating body of Virginia. Then the ships returned, this time filled with rondos, sonnets, madrigals, odes, books of fables and parodies that resisted the successive snows. I am now surrounded by whales and moose, by a flock of seagulls; I enter into the torment of shapes, swimming suddenly in my rising desire to see, between my lips, my tongue slipping on the very tender flesh of the word clitoris. *Breathe your silence, respira en tu memoria*, impregnate rhetoric. In history and the present I am shaping the subjectivity of her whose mouth resembles mine.

fait de langue tourmente
rattrape-moi dans ma tradition
dans la durée de la phrase
le plaisir en douceur espacé
rattrape-moi dans ma différence

fact of tongue torments
catch hold of me in my tradition
in the timespan of a phrase
pleasure spaced gently
catch up to me in my difference

Translated by Robert Majzels and Erín Moure

une fois reproduites dans la langue
nos blessures réciproques forment
des œuvres de la taille d'un oui
comme dans certains tableaux
où les bouches font des boucles
de mémoire avec la douleur
la parfaite lumière
du matin qui pénètre larghetto
dans la voix

once reproduced in language
our reciprocal wounds form
works huge as a yes
as in certain paintings
where the mouths are loops
of memory shaped by sorrow
perfect light
of morning that penetrates
larghetto in the voice

Translated by Robert Majzels and Erín Moure

une façon de se jeter sur le lit pour que le corps
exerce sa joie oui j'ai souvent pensé que selon les
climats la lumière nous dessinait une âme
surprenante au fond du regard, des roses abon-
damment, et en même temps pour mieux nous
éclairer sur le plaisir, j'ai longtemps cru que la
lumière en nous renversant d'un souffle rendait
nos pensées si souples que nous pouvions,
goûtant l'étreinte et le climat, changer de corps et
d'identité

a way of flopping on the bed so the body exerts its joy yes
I've often thought that depending on the weather the light
sketched us a startling soul deep in the gaze, roses
abundant, and at the same time to enlighten us on pleasure I
thought for ages that in knocking us over with a breath the
light made our thoughts so supple we could taste the
embrace and weather, alter bodies and selves

Translated by Robert Majzels and Erín Moure

ce sont toujours les mêmes mots
grands objets de paroles
lumière nuit ou silence
les mêmes oiseaux l'après-midi
le bruit de l'automne un autre
paragraphe en deçà des mots
quand je respire
la réponse qui fuit

they are always the same words
large spoken objects
light night or silence
the same birds the afternoon
the sound of autumn another
paragraph on the intimate side of words
when I breathe
the fleeting response

aujourd'hui je sais que la structure la plus bleue
de la mer se rapproche de nos cellules et de la
souffrance intouchable comme la vie fait trois fois
le tour de notre enfance sans jamais y toucher
vraiment parce qu'on est proche de la réalité et
que la matière ne peut pas tomber sans nous
avertir, nous laisser là, la peau hésitante entre les
philosophies et l'aube, à moitié, à jamais dans le
tourment, dans la vaste complication de la beauté

today I know that the deepest blue structure of the sea comes close to our cells and untouchable suffering as life circles around our childhood three times without ever really touching it because we are close to reality and matter cannot fall without warning us, leaving us there, skin hesitating between philosophies and the dawn, halfway, forever in torment, in the vast complication of beauty

Théâtre: vitesse d'eau

l'univers est dans la page à la page
suivante
comme l'aube efface la nuit
l'eau a lavé le ciel puis on a dit
que l'encre avait fui emportant avec elle
les écailles et les antennes
tout le système de reproduction
la nudité des êtres de raison

Theatre. Speed of Water

the universe is on the page one page
over
as dawn erases night
water has washed the sky and we said
the ink fled carrying with it
husks and antennae
the whole system of reproduction
the nudity of reasoning beings

ce soir si tu rapproches ton visage
et que la civilisation s'étire
au bout de tes bras, ce soir
si en plein vol tu rattrapes mon image
dis que c'était au loin
comme un dé dans la nuit

tonight if you lean your face close
and civilization stretches out
at the end of your arms, tonight
if in full flight you catch my image
say it was from afar
like a die in the night

Palmiers. Le présent n'est pas un livre

à cause du corps le sens de la vie
change constamment vertige
car si l'océan était à l'autre bout du destin
un éclat de vert
délicat travail de présence
à l'intention d'une humanité nomade
le futur et le futur s'emmêleraient

or le présent vient vite
à chaque phrase une nouvelle configuration
du sens où personne n'hésite
en pensée en ivresse
le présent n'est pas un livre
joie qui traverse les rosiers

Palm Trees. The Present Is Not a Book

because of the body the meaning of life
constantly changes vertigo
for if the ocean were at the far end of destiny
spark of green
delicate work of presence
intended for a nomad humanity
the future and the future would run together

yet the present comes swiftly
with each phrase a new configuration
of meaning where no one hesitates
in thought in rapture
the present is not a book
joy that traverses the rosebushes

Le silence de l'hibiscus

l'âme des gens je l'ai longtemps cherchée
dans les angles morts du plaisir
et quelques promesses tournées tournesols
vers une meilleure définition de la douleur
l'âme des gens il m'arrivait de la dessiner
grand jeu d'ombre tracée espérance de vie

The Silence of the Hibiscus

the soul of people I've long searched for it
in the blind spots of pleasure
and a few promises sunflowers spun
toward a better definition of pain
the soul of people occasionally I drew it
trace of great shadow play expectancy of life

Wanuskewin

6 février 1999

à Louise Forsyth

la blancheur toute l'immensité
vallons de culture et d'horizon
le silence caresse nos joues
les tipis en peau de bison
triangles de chaleur au loin dans la plaine

caméras en mains
nous cadrons dans l'imaginaire
un troupeau de bisons sa chute
au bas de la falaise
masses de chair et filets de vie
le bruit de l'inconnu
soleil indien entre les paupières
nous laissons filer le temps
l'histoire au-dessus de nos têtes
les « chiennes du soleil » vont
vers l'approche bleue de l'été et des baies

Wanuskewin
February 6, 1999

for Louise Forsyth

whiteness total immensity
vales of culture and horizon
silence caresses our cheeks
buffalo-skin teepees
triangles of warmth in the distance on the plain

cameras in hand
we frame in imagination
a herd of bison its jump
to the bottom of the cliff
masses of flesh and strands of life
sound of the unknown
indian summer through eyelids
we let time flow
history above our heads
the "sun-dogs" are moving
toward the blue approach of summer and berries

Hôtel Clarendon

Québec, mai 2000

ce serait un extrait de roman
avec du jazz et des martinis
dans le miroir il y aurait des objets
des visages. Tu embrasserais l'épaule
d'une femme son regard nu
et le fleuve tu parlerais du fleuve
de l'été sur la rue Saint-Jean en marchant
tu décrirais je t'aime et le continent
tu ferais semblant de vivre là

Hotel Clarendon

Quebec, May, 2000

it would be an excerpt from a novel
with jazz and martinis
in the mirror there would be objects
faces. You would embrace the shoulder
of a woman her naked stare
and the river you would speak of the river
of summer while walking on rue Saint-Jean
you would describe I love you and the continent
you would make believe you live there

Ogunquit
15 septembre 2001

une lueur ancienne dans les yeux des Atrides
on prépare la guerre
ne laisse pas l'obscurité   s'installer
seul le verbe vie   décide
si nous nous consumerons devant la mer
si cette vie vaut de s'enflammer
au milieu des dunes et des quartz
maintenant que la nuit a délogé les horloges
et les métaphores

Ogunquit
September 15, 2001

an ancient glint in Atridae eyes
preparing war
don't let obscurity set in
only the verb life   decide
if we will consume ourselves before the sea
if this life is worth setting ourselves on fire
in the middle of dunes and quartz
now that night has dislodged clocks
and metaphors

Suggestions le coeur serré

1.
l'idée de se balancer au bout d'un je
suspendu
aux joies fiévreuses de juillet
ou salivant devant l'obscur
d'un présent rempli de
pourquoi qui ruissellent dans les pensées

2.
alors fais-moi le plaisir
de tracer des mots impossibles à trouer
remonte le cours du temps
entre les dialogues ne vacille pas

3.
répète: la mémoire
tiens bon. La langue
elle veut
de nous, de tout
se lover partout se nourrir
du silence

4.
une idée d'absolu
emportée d'un mot d'un coup
par le vent
pose ta question

Suggestions Heavy-Hearted

1
the idea of balancing on the tip of an I
suspended
by the feverish joys of July
or salivating before the dark
of a present filled with
whys that stream through thoughts

2
then give me the pleasure
of tracing words impossible to tear holes in
go back through the course of time
between dialogues don't waver

3
repeat: memory
hold fast. The tongue
it calls
on us, on everything
curls up everywhere to feed
on silence

4
an idea of absolute
carried off in a word in a blast
of wind
ask your question

Soft Link 2

Mais il y a dehors, le froid la chaleur la violence pliée en deux de douleur dans de beaux draps aux abords des villes et des forêts, il y a dehors et c'est pire chaque fois puisqu'il y a va-et-vient d'armes, vendeurs de femmes et d'enfants, hommes à chemise blanche qui tripotent nos gènes et nos cellules comme des marchandises. Aussi, j'ai idée qu'il faut être au monde souvent et parcourir en moins de deux temps tous les ici et ailleurs du désir, aller de là à jadis ou demain comme un chamois qui fait son essuie-glace sur le dos de l'univers. Mais il y a dehors et on dirait qu'il en résulte un monde difficile à vivre malgré la luminosité des brises tropicales de décembre. Dedans, il y a des mots qui nous permettent d'inventer, de tisser de ces ficelles qui ont tout pour nous suspendre à la force des poignets et nous aider à balancer le corps. Dehors il y a dehors avec des horizons, des raccourcis, d'étranges peurs qui se renouvellent à même le corps et ses envies d'envol, mais il y a dehors comme à la chasse avec des proies, des plombs, des royaumes, des identités cachées sous les vêtements; il y a les cimetières, les bars à gogo, les zones de sécurité, des lois spéciales. Dehors si on touche au côté vivant des choses, le beau côté tournant de vie déploie facilement ses roses, ses blancs lumineux qui traversent la voix des enfants, leurs bras rieurs. Mais il y a dehors où le côté vivant de la souffrance n'apparaît jamais. Puis tu t'endors sur le nom des choses publiques oubliant l'obscurité qui traverse facilement la vie, la buée dans les yeux qui rassemble les os au nord des tempes comme des fruits, des jouets, des mots avec leurs angles de genoux de coudes et de noix qui défilent en réponses ou brisent et transforment les mots de l'ombre ceux qui accélèrent le pouls et modulent encore et encore des frissons le tressaillement des bêtes. Mais il y a dehors il y a la durée de l'errance. Dehors l'aube savante s'enroule dans le temps.

Soft Link 2

But there's outside, the cold the heat the violence dou-
bled over in pain in a real bind at the edge of city and
forest, there's outside and it's worse each time as there's
traffic of weapons, traders of women and children,
white-shirted men who manipulate our genes and cells
like so much merchandise. And it seems to me we have
to be in the world often and in a flash traverse all the to-
and-fro of desire, go from there to long ago or tomor-
row like a chamois on a windshield swiping across the
back of the universe. But there's outside and you might
say as a result the world's hard to take despite the
December luminosity of tropical breezes. Inside, words
let us invent, weave cords strong enough to hang by
our wrists and help balance the body. Outside there's
outside with horizons, shortcuts, strange fears reborn
in the body and its desire to take flight, but there's out-
side like hunting with prey, pellets, kingdoms, identi-
ties hidden under clothes; there are cemeteries, discos,
security zones, war measures. Outside if we touch the
living face of things, the beautiful face all spun with life
easily unfurls its roses, its luminous whites that traverse
children's voices, their laughing arms. But there's out-
side where the living face of suffering never shows. So
you fall asleep on the name of public things, forgetting
the darkness that runs easily through life, the blur in
the eyes that gathers bones north of the forehead like
fruits, toys, words with their angled knees and elbows
and the tree nuts that parade in answer or that smash
and transform shadow words those that race the pulse
and modulate again and again the tremours of beasts
and shivers. But there's outside there's the duration of
wandering. Outside the knowing dawn coils in time.

dans le temps facile et bleu
quand la lumière est lente
et fait des noeuds de toute urgence
avec les ombres et les catastrophes
tu dis qu'il faut de la pluie
de la pluie et encore plus de nuit
que ne peut l'abîme
ou le silence des gens de tendresse

in a time blue and easy
when the light is slow
and ties urgent knots
with shadow and catastrophe
you say we need rain
rain and even more night
than the abyss can rein in
or the silence of people of tenderness

tiens-toi bien dans le silence
à l'aube le verbe être court vite
dans les veines, corps céleste il file
comme après l'amour ou grain de sel
sur la langue le matin, goût d'immensité
ou lumière dans la déferle du temps
il rapproche
de l'humidité première
viens m'embrasser
pense au grand pouvoir de l'eau
qui fait de nous un lieu

hold on in silence
at dawn the verb to be courses
in the veins, a heavenly body, it flies
as after love or grain of salt
on the tongue early morning, taste of immensity
it draws near
the first dampness
come kiss me
think of the great power of water
that makes a place of us

Le dos indocile des mots

lèvres lilas longtemps
liqueur de lumière et de littérature
ou petit lézard de Lido (n.m. cordon littoral en position
avancée à l'entrée d'une baie et pouvant isoler une lagune)
lové dans mon lexique-lion de questions

au bord des lèvres lesbiennes longtemps
libre de larmes sous l'azur lapis-lazuli
je me languis d'un goût de lobe doux et de loukoum
longtemps je fis cette lecture
de lagune et de langue lointaines lyriques

The Indocile Back of Words

long-time lilac lips
liquor of light and literature
or little lizard of the Lido (n. long sandbar at the mouth of a
bay that shelters a lagoon)
louvered in my lion-lexicon of questions

long-time on lesbian lips
let loose from tears under lapis-lazuli light
I long to lick sweet lobe and loukoum
long-time I leaned into this reading
of lyric lagoon and language long ago

Translated by Robert Majzels and Erín Moure

Le dos indocile des mots

pour toutes les passions au présent
parfois une promenade
nous plongions dans le paysage
avec des phrases, des pensées
au pouvoir de parfum et de paradoxe
parfois
la poussière. On la disait de Pékin de Palmyre
ou de Pompéi
nous la partagions à plein poumon
on parlait de physiquement posséder
la poésie

The Indocile Back of Words

for all the passions in the present
possible a promenade
we plunged into panoramas
with phrases, ponderings
to the power of perfume and paradox
possibly
particles of dust. Say it's from Peking or Palmyra
or Pompey
we partook in its plenitude
proposed to physically possess
poetry

Translated by Robert Majzels and Erín Moure

Postface

Quelle que soit la tristesse ou la mélancolie que nous portons en nous, je doute que l'on puisse écrire de la poésie sans un acquiescement à la vie, sans un enthousiasme et un emportement capables de nous arracher à la réalité et paradoxalement de nous donner la compréhension intuitive des énigmes qui en font la complexité. Le poème est toujours une histoire de ferveur qui oscille entre le plaisir des mots et une intuition forte et renouvelée de la vie.

Autant j'aime dans mes romans changer d'identité, cultiver l'étrangeté, autant je suis, en poésie, fidèle à ce que je suis en pensée, en désir et en imagination. La poésie est pour moi un consentement à la vie qui nourrit, module et renouvelle mon rapport à la réalité. La langue m'incite toujours à passer à l'action. Selon l'énergie, les émotions, les sensations, elle se transforme, tendue, vigilante ou ludique. À long terme, ces variations auront animé les tons et les traits de ma poésie. Un peu comme les traits d'un même visage varient selon l'éclairage et selon le sentiment. Bien sûr, il y a des états d'âme dans l'existence (amour, deuil, mélancolie, désir fou) qui altèrent ponctuellement en renforçant ou en modifiant la singularité d'une écriture. Par exemple, *Amantes* est un recueil écrit en état de limerance et d'amour, tout comme *L'aviva* affirme les premiers moments de mon intérêt pour la traduction non seulement comme un jeu de variations possibles au cœur du sens et de la valeur, mais aussi comme courant souterrain d'étrangeté devant l'insaisissable. De même, *Si Sismal* témoigne-t-il de cet état d'esprit. Quant aux traductions inédites du *Centre blanc* par Barbara Godard, elles relancent à mes yeux le souffle troublant d'une *imponctuation* nécessaire et désirée pour traduire et rassembler le vide, le blanc, la respiration, la mort, l'énergie, tous mots qui, dans ma langue, m'apparaissaient intraduisibles. Il m'arrive aussi de penser que la *traduction fiction* est, en tant que pratique ludique et motrice de glissements de sens, une « suite logique » aux questions posées par le duo réalité/fiction revu et corrigé par la conscience féministe.

Je suis touchée par la lecture de *Mobility of Light* parce que cette anthologie me fait voir en quelques pages comment j'ai traversé l'espace collectif et singulier. Elle me permet d'avoir une vue d'ensemble sur ce que j'appelle, par contraste avec la biographie, ma bio-sémantique ainsi que sur ce qui constitue les nœuds de ferveur d'une vie d'écriture; elle me permet aussi d'entendre *le grain d'une voix* [1] qui ressemble à la mienne. Car on aura sans doute repéré dans cette

Afterword

Whatever the sadness or melancholy we carry around with us might be, I doubt that it is possible to write poetry without an acquiescence to life, without enthusiasm, without zeal. These are needed to rip us out of reality and, paradoxically, to give us the intuitive comprehension required to understand the enigmas that comprise its complexity. The poem is always an event of fervour that oscillates between the pleasure of words and a powerful and renewed intuition of life.

Much as I like to change identity and cultivate strangeness in my novels, I am, in poetry, faithful to myself in thought, in desire and in imagination. For me, poetry is a consent to life, to life which nourishes, modulates and renews my relation to reality. Language always incites me to take action. Depending upon the energy, the emotions, the sensations, it transforms itself: taut, vigilant or ludic. Over the long term, it has been these variations that brought life to the tones and traits of my poetry. A bit as the features of the same face can vary depending upon the lighting and the feeling. Of course, existence alters the states of the soul (love, grief, melancholy, passion) at particular moments in time when it reinforces or produces change in the uniqueness of a writing style. For example, *Amantes* is a collection written in a state of limerance and love, just as *L'aviva* affirms the first moments of my interest in translation, not only as a game of possible variations at the heart of meaning and value, but also as a subterranean current of strangeness when confronted with the elusive. *Si sismal* is also evidence for such a state of mind. The unpublished translations of *Le centre blanc* by Barbara Godard pick up the ball once again in my eyes on the disturbing rustle produced by an *absence of punctuation* that is both necessary and desired if one is to translate and bring together the void, white, breath, death, all words which, in my language, appeared untranslatable to me. In addition, there are times when I think that *fictive translation* is, as a ludic practice and generator of shifts in sense, a "suite logic" for the questions raised by the duo reality/fiction as it has been revisioned and corrected by feminist consciousness.

I am touched when I read *Mobility of Light* because this anthology shows me in a few pages how I have traversed personal and collective space. It allows me to take an overview of what I am calling, in contrast with biography, my bio-semiology, as well as what makes up the nodes of fervour in a life of writing. In

anthologie comment l'excessive, la rationnelle, l'insoumise et l'exploratrice que je suis[2] ont nourri et orchestré le paysage des questions et des emportements qu'il m'a semblé nécessaire de partager dans la langue et son pouvoir poétique. C'est en ce sens que, quelle que soit la manière d'être d'un écrivain, l'essentiel est de saisir en quoi sa grammaire et sa syntaxe personnelles contribuent à faire vibrer, réfléchir, à déstabiliser, à faire rêver. On dit depuis toujours que la poésie est en dehors de toute finalité et que c'est cela qui lui assure sa liberté de mouvement. C'est vrai, tout au moins, il est bon de le penser mais je ne peux pas effacer l'idée d'une sismographie témoignant de l'énergie singulière taillant dans la langue des relais de sens et d'espoir. Dans mon cas, ces relais auront été, le corps, la ville, la conscience féministe, l'utopie et le désir lesbiens, ma fascination pour l'acte d'écriture (langue, traduction, virtualité du langage), l'art et le voyage, et toutes les questions nouvelles surgies de la civilisation de « l'individualisme de masse » dans son aspect le plus marchand, le plus simpliste, le plus rapide.

Mobility of Light traverse quatre décennies d'écriture. Dès le tout premier poème du premier recueil publié, la poésie est associée à un espace de lumière. Elle abonde en éclats de sens qui la rapprochent du chaud sensuel. Certes, entre les années 1968 et 1974, elle se confondra avec l'idée de texte, son neutre rêvé comme scientifique et explorateur dont on verra les traces dans *L'écho bouge beau, Suite logique, Le centre blanc, Mécanique jongleuse et Masculin grammaticale*, voire même dans *Marginal Way*. Phénomène intéressant, ces textes « neutralisés » ne seront pas de froideur mais apparaîtront comme un contre-chant sensuel, érotique et philosophique, du moins je l'espère. Il y a dans ma pratique du texte un immense désir de comprendre, de déjouer et de transgresser l'organisation du sens. J'y vois aussi une intention de se faire plaisir par un usage extravagant des mots. Plus tard, l'idée de texte trouvera sa forme en rencontrant des « idées de prose ». Je songe ici à *L'amèr*, à *La partie pour le tout*, à certains poèmes d'*Amantes* ainsi qu'au recueil *Langues obscures*.

En ce qui concerne la prose poétique je crois qu'il y aurait un travail intéressant à faire en regardant de plus près à quel moment la prose poétique et la poésie en prose s'insinuent dans l'aura du poème, s'avèrent nécessaires, à l'écriture du poème. Le poète français René Daumal disait : « La prose parle de quelque chose, la poésie fait quelque chose par des paroles ». Pourquoi ce besoin soudain de vouloir parler de quelque chose, de « normaliser » l'expression, la phrase, à tout le moins, de donner l'impression de respecter la convention syntaxique ? À quel moment doit-on cesser de dire poème pour introduire le concept de poème en prose ou de prose poétique ? Pour ma part, j'ai toujours associé la prose au quotidien qui est, somme toute, notre rapport obligé au réel ; de même que je n'ai cessé d'affirmer que la prose romanesque me servait à négocier avec le réel. En fait, j'ai souvent pensé que la prose, si fréquente dans le poème au féminin des années 75 et 85,

addition, it allows me to hear *the grain of the voice* [1] which resembles mine. For, undoubtedly, readers will already have noticed in this anthology how the extravagance, rationality, unruliness and love of exploration that make me who I am [2] have nourished and orchestrated the landscape of questions and upheavals which it seemed necessary to me to share in language and its poetic power. It is in this sense that, whatever might be writers' manner of being, the main thing is to seize the ways in which their personal syntax and grammar generate vibration, reflection, destabilization and dreams. It has been said since time immemorial that poetry is outside all finality and that is what ensures its freedom of movement. This is true, at least it is good to think so, but I am unable to erase the idea of a seismography providing evidence for the unique energy that carves markers of meaning and hope in language. In my case, these markers will have been the body, the city, feminist consciousness, lesbian utopia and desire, my fascination with the act of writing (language, translation, virtuality of linguistic expression), art and journeys, and all the new questions that have surged forth out of civilization's "spirit of mass *it's-all-about-meism*" in its most market-based, simplistic and fast aspects.

Mobility of Light traverses four decades of writing. Right from the very first poem of the first published collection, poetry is associated with a space of light. It abounds in shards of sense by which it draws close to sensual warmth. Certainly, between the years 1968 and 1974, it is intermingled with the idea of *text*, [3] its neutrality dreamt as scientific and exploratory. Traces of this can be seen in *L'écho bouge beau, Suite logique, Le centre blanc, Mécanique jongleuse et Masculin grammaticale*, indeed even in *Marginal Way*. An interesting phenomenon: these "neutralized" texts would not have been seen as cold, but appeared to be a philosophical, erotic and sensual counter-melody, at least I hope this is the case. There is in my practice of text an immense desire to understand, to thwart and to transgress the organization of meaning. I also see in it an intention to give oneself pleasure through an extravagant use of words. Later, the idea of text found its form through encountering "prose ideas." I am thinking here of *L'amèr, La partie pour le tout*, certain poems in *Amantes*, as well as the collection *Langues obscures*.

As far as poetic prose is concerned, I believe it would be an interesting project to take a close look at the moment when poetic prose and prose poetry insinuated themselves into the aura of the poem, proved themselves necessary to the writing of the poem. The French poet René Daumal said: "Prose speaks about something, poetry does something through words." Why was there this sudden need to speak about something, to "normalize" expression, the sentence, at the very least, to give the impression of respecting syntactic convention? At what moment must one cease to say poem in order to introduce the concept of prose poem or poetic

servait à la vraie vie, cachait un besoin de « petite histoire » au milieu d'emportements ayant pour conséquence une dé-figuration de la norme linguistique (cette désobéissance majeure qu'est le poème) suivie d'une reconfiguration du sens. Ce phénomène de dé-figuration est propre au poème. Ainsi peut-on dire que le poème en prose aurait servi de « garde-folie » contre un écart à la norme, perçu comme trop dangereux; de même le poème en prose aurait aussi permis au sujet féminin d'infiltrer d'un même mouvement la poésie et le texte, l'un et l'autre offrant des zones intimes et publiques, des temps de silence et d'histoire.

Ce phénomène de dé-figuration et de reconfiguration, je le retrouve aussi aujourd'hui chez de jeunes poètes à un moment de l'histoire où le réel, le fictif et le virtuel travaillent ex-æquo à nourrir simultanément le sens et le non-sens, phénomène dont nous avons peu à peu appris à nous servir pour échapper à une impossible résolution d'images et de valeurs qui caractérisent aujourd'hui le politique et l'éthique d'une société essentiellement marchande.

À partir du recueil *Installations,* il m'a semblé entrer dans un nouvel espace de présence et de questionnement. Je crois que l'inquiétude trouble qui accompagne les différentes installations de mots est annonciatrice des questions de civilisation qui surgiront dans mes textes de prose et de poésie à partir de 1995 avec *Baroque d'aube, Musée de l'os et de l'eau, Hier, Cahier de roses et de civilisation* et tout récemment avec *Après les mots.* En effet, à partir des années 95, soit cinq ans avant de changer de siècle et de millénaire, au moment où se mettent en place les grands axes de la mondialisation et des nouvelles technologies et que commencent à se faire sentir leurs effets sur les dualités traditionnelles et répertoriées de l'humanisme tels le vrai et le faux, le bien et le mal, ainsi que sur les évidentes contraintes de l'espace et du temps, de la reproduction, de l'origine, de la vieillesse, de notre rapport à la nature, de nouvelles propositions vont surgir dans l'espace éthique jusqu'alors circonscrit par les vieilles et valables questions philosophiques posées par l'Occident.

Des mots tels espèce, gène, humanité, siècle et civilisation viendront chasser le vocabulaire de l'utopie et du désir, sans pour autant effacer les mots *futur* et *beauté* qui de tout temps nous ont parlé à travers les grands symboles de la nuit, de la lumière, de la mer et du vent, du soleil et de la pluie, de la nuque, de l'œil, et de la bouche, du bleu, du rouge et du rose, du noir et du blanc. Et tout ce temps, je suis là, vigilante, attentive à réunir des mots comme le temps, les os, l'art et la beauté, à vouloir comprendre où est notre bonheur, où se forment les larmes et les métaphores concernant l'intelligence de notre espèce ainsi que la violence impitoyable des figures archaïques et marchandes de cette même espèce.

Mais il y a la langue, sa virtualité incommensurable qui fait en grande partie le plaisir des mots. Et tout recommence. Sur *Le dos indocile des mots* s'annonce

prose? For my part, I have always associated prose with daily life, with that which is, in the final analysis, our obligatory connection to the real; similarly, I have never ceased affirming that novelistic prose worked for me in negotiating with the real. In fact, I have often thought that prose, so frequent in poems in the feminine during the years 1975 to 1985, served real life, concealed a need for "life stories" in the midst of upheavals that were working to de-figure linguistic norms (that major disobedience which is the poem) and then to reconfigure meaning. This phenomenon of de-figuration is unique to the poem. Thus, we can say that the prose poem served as a "mad-guard" protecting against a departure from the norm, seen as too dangerous. In the same way, the prose poem could also be said to have allowed the feminine subject to infiltrate with a single stroke both poem and text, one and the other offering intimate and public zones, tracks of silence and participation in the human parade.

I also find this phenomenon of de-figuration and reconfiguration today in young poets at a moment in history when the real, the fictional and the virtual are tied for first place as they are working to feed sense and nonsense simultaneously. It is a phenomenon we have gradually learned to use for ourselves in untangling the impossible concatenation of images and values that characterize the political and the ethical in today's essentially market-based society.

At the time of the collection *Installations*, it seemed to me that I was entering a new space of presence and questioning. I believe that the turbid disquiet which accompanies the different word installations anticipates the questions about civilization which would appear in my prose and poetry texts starting in 1995 with *Baroque d'aube*, then *Musée de l'os et de l'eau, Hier, Cahier de roses et de civilisation* and just recently *Après les mots*. In effect, from 1995 on, that is five years before changing century and millennium, at the moment when the big axes of globalization and new technologies were setting themselves up and their effects beginning to make themselves felt on the catalogued and traditional dualities of humanism, such as true and false, good and evil, as well as the obvious constraints of space and time, reproduction, origin, aging, our relation with nature, new propositions were starting to surge forth into the ethical space which had previously been circumscribed by the old and valid philosophical questions raised by the West.

Words such as species, gene, humanity, century and civilization arrived and chased away the vocabulary of utopia and desire, without for all that erasing the words *future* and *beauty* which for all time have spoken to us through the great symbols of night, light, the sea and the wind, the sun and the rain, the nape of the neck, the eye, mouth, blue, red and pink, black and white. And all this time, I am there, vigilant, attentive to bringing words together like time, bones, art and beauty, to trying to understand where our happiness lies, where tears and

un autre voyage d'*Ardeur* au milieu des êtres d'appétit et de mélancolie que nous sommes, au milieu des villes dangereuses, de la planète trop chaude et du cosmos fascinant.

Oui, je parlerai longtemps encore « de physiquement posséder la poésie »[3] dans la mobilité de la lumière.

—*Nicole Brossard*
15 juillet 2008, 11h

Notes

1 Allusion au titre d'un livre de Roland Barthes: *Le grain de la voix.*
2 *L'horizon du fragment* paru aux Éditions Trois-Pistoles, 2004.
3 Nicole Brossard in *Après les mots*, page 52.

metaphors form concerning the intelligence of our species as well as the pitiless violence of the merchant and archaic figures of this same species.

But there is language, its incommensurable virtuality which creates in large part the pleasure of words. And everything begins again. On *The indocile back of words* another journey of *Ardour* can be foreseen in the midst of the melancholic and desiring beings that we are, in the midst of dangerous cities, of the too hot planet and of the fascinating cosmos.

Yes, I will be speaking for a long time yet of "physically possessing poetry"[4] in the mobility of light.

—*Nicole Brossard*
July 15, 2008, 11 A.M.

Notes

1 Allusion to the title of a book by Roland Barthes: *Le Grain de la voix.*
2 See *L'horizon du fragment.*
3 The text is a thoughtful reflective approach to the process of writing and reading. "[...] To write a text, you only need a 'motive' to trigger the pleasure of writing and to perform or to explore in language" ("Poetic Politics," in *Fluid Arguments*, page 36).
4 Nicole Brossard in *Après les mots*, 52.

Acknowledgements

Louise H. Forsyth wishes to express her warm thanks to all the translators whose work appears in this volume. The alacrity and enthusiasm with which they agreed to allow their already published translations to be included was heart-warming. It was also pure joy to collaborate with those who were willing, without hesitation, to do translations specifically for this project and to set aside other priorities in order to exchange ideas with Brossard and Forsyth and then meet deadlines. Together, these many translators form a team of artists in language whose creative and ludic work with language has played and continues to play a vital role in the widening ripples of influence of Brossard's inspiring texts and of poetry itself.

*

Poems from *Aube à la saison, Mordre en sa chair, L'écho bouge beau, Suite logique, Le centre blanc, Mécanique jongleuse,* suivi de *Masculin grammaticale,* and *La partie pour le tout* © 1978 by Nicole Brossard and Les Éditions de l'Hexagone. Reprinted with permission from Les Éditions de l'Hexagone. English translation © 1980 Nicole Brossard for poems from *Daydream Mechanics.*

Excerpt from *L'amèr ou le chapitre effrité* © 1984 Nicole Brossard and Les Éditions de l'Hexagone. Reprinted with permission from Les Éditions de l'Hexagone. English translation *These Our Mothers Or: The Disintegrating Chapter* © 1983 Barbara Godard and Nicole Brossard. Reprinted with permission from Barbara Godard.

Poems from *Amantes* © 1998 Nicole Brossard and Les Éditions de l'Hexagone. Reprinted with permission from Les Éditions de l'Hexagone. English translation *Lovhers* © Barbara Godard and Guernica Editions. Reprinted with permission from Guernica Editions and Barbara Godard.

"Marginal Way," published in *Double Impression,* © 1984 Nicole Brossard and Les Éditions de l'Hexagone. Reprinted with permission from Les Éditions de l'Hexagone.

Poems from *L'aviva* © 1985 Nicole Brossard. Reprinted with permission from Nicole Brossard. Poems from *L'aviva / Aviva* © 2008. Reprinted with permission from Nicole Brossard and Anne-Marie Wheeler.

"Si sismal," published in *À tout regard*, © 1989 Nicole Brossard and Bibliothèque québécoise. Reprinted with permission from Bibliothèque québécoise and Nicole Brossard. English translation "If Yes Seismal" © Nicole Brossard and Fred Wah. Reprinted with permission from Nicole Brossard and Fred Wah.

Poems from *Installations (avec ou sans pronoms)* © 1989 Nicole Brossard and Les Écrits des Forges. Reprinted with permission from Nicole Brossard and Les Écrits des Forges. English translations *Installations (with or without pronouns)* © Nicole Brossard, Robert Majzels, Erín Moure, The Muses Company. Reprinted with permission from Nicole Brossard, Robert Majzels, Erín Moure, and The Muses Co./ J. Gordon Shillingford Publishing.

Poems from *Langues obscures* © 1992 Nicole Brossard and Les Éditions de l'Hexagone. Reprinted with permission from Nicole Brossard and Les Éditions de l'Hexagone.

Poem from *La nuit verte du Parc Labyrinthe* © 1992 Nicole Brossard. Reprinted with permission from Nicole Brossard. English translation *Green Night of Labyrinth Park* © Nicole Brossard and Lou Nelson. Reprinted with permission from Nicole Brossard and Lou Nelson.

Poems from *Vertige de l'avant-scène* © 1997 Nicole Brossard and Les Écrits des Forges. Reprinted with permission from Nicole Brossard and Les Écrits des Forges.

Poems from *Au présent des veines* © 1999 Nicole Brossard and Les Écrits des Forges. Reprinted with permission from Nicole Brossard and Les Écrits des Forges.

Poems from *Musée de l'os et de l'eau* © 1999 Nicole Brossard and Les Éditions du Noroît. Reprinted with permission from Nicole Brossard and Les Éditions du Noroît. English translation *Museum of Bone and Water* © 2003 by Nicole Brossard, Robert Majzels, Erín Moure, and House of Anansi Press. Reprinted with permission from Nicole Brossard, Robert Majzels, Erín Moure, and House of Anansi Press.

Poems from *Je m'en vais à Trieste* © 2003 Nicole Brossard and Les Écrits des Forges. Reprinted with permission from Nicole Brossard and Les Écrits des Forges.

Poems from *Cahier de roses et de civilisation* © 2003 Nicole Brossard and Les Éditions d'Art Le Sabord. Reprinted with permission from Nicole Brossard and Les Éditions d'Art Le Sabord. English translation *Notebook of Roses and Civilization* © 2007 Nicole Brossard, Robert Majzels, Erín Moure, and Coach House Books. Reprinted with permission from Nicole Brossard, Robert Majzels, Erín Moure, and Coach House Books.

lps Books in the Laurier Poetry Series
Published by Wilfrid Laurier University Press

Don McKay *Field Marks: The Poetry of Don McKay*, edited by Méira Cook, with an afterword by Don McKay • 2006 • xxvi + 60 pp. • ISBN-10: 0-88920-494-2; ISBN-13: 978-0-88920-494-2

Al Purdy *The More Easily Kept Illusions: The Poetry of Al Purdy*, edited by Robert Budde, with an afterword by Russell Brown • 2006 • xvi + 80 pp. • ISBN-10: 0-88920-490-X; ISBN-13: 978-0-88920-490-4